The Coffee Break Guide to Social Media for Writers

HOW TO SUCCEED ON SOCIAL MEDIA AND STILL HAVE TIME TO WRITE

Amy Denim

Coffee Break Publishing

DENVER, COLORADO

Coffee Break Publishing
www.coffeebreaksocialmedia.com

Book Layout ©2013 BookDesignTemplates.com

Ordering Information:
Quantity sales. Special discounts are available on quantity purchases by corporations, associations, and others. For details, contact the "Special Sales Department" at the address above.

The Coffee Break Guide to Social Media for Writers: How to Succeed on Social Media and Still Have Time to Write/ Amy Denim.—1st ed.
ISBN – 13: 978-0615925301
ISBN – 10: 0615925308

Dedication

*For the members of Colorado Romance Writers
without whom I never would have thought to write non-
fiction books for authors.*

And for my dad,

who always believed in every word I ever wrote.

Acknowledgements

This book would not have been possible without some amazing people in my life who believed in me and the ideas floating around in my head and my laptop.

Special thanks to my Beta readers, Larie Brannick, and Jennifer Maitlen. So glad we all get to tweet now (even when we're sitting right next to each other).

I can't thank Diane Whiddon at Novel Website Design enough for designing CoffeeBreakSocialMedia.com, helping with the cover, and especially for her encouragement to put my social media knowledge to good use.

Pictures are worth a thousand words, so here's a thousand thanks to Mike Sands at 3M&H Design for all his graphics help with covers and Facebook and websites, oh my!

A great big thank you to my editors Shannnon Janeczek and Ahuva Rogers. They are grammar and punctuation royalty, so any mistakes remaining in this book soooooo belong to me.

Contents

CHAPTER 1

The Social Media Monster

Don't Let Social Media Scare You

When I first got serious about writing, I joined a local writing group. Best idea I ever had. They've given me so much support from day one. I highly recommend this step for anyone who wants to make a go at writing and selling his or her work.

One of the first events my group put on after I joined was a writers' retreat. We went up to the mountains, got all inspired by the wildlife, the scenery, and the hot tub. There may also have been some wine involved. Good times.

We spent a chunk of the weekend putting words on the page. But, we also had a few guest speakers to boost our morale and inspire our writing. One of our presenters was an editor from a small, but growing, press. Her topic was query letters, but as writers and editors tend to do, we moved off like a rocket on a tangent.

Social media.

And it scared the living nightlife out of me.

She threw around words like platform, followers, tweet, and discoverability. This big bad scary editor said I should have my platform established two years before I submitted anything. Ahhhh!

I didn't even know what a platform was, much less how to create one online. I wasn't on Twitter, I'd never heard of Goodreads, Pinterest was just a funny word, and the only time I spent on Facebook was to take weird surveys, play farming games, and tag pictures of my drunken friends.

But, if I wanted to be a published author, it seemed I needed to do more than just write. Who knew?

This relaxing weekend in the mountains left me in need of some meditation and a massage. But I skipped the yoga and went out and bought a smartphone instead.

I spent the next year becoming a social media fiend. And I barely finished one manuscript. I had created an online presence, but I had diddly-squat to pitch. Oops.

The purpose of writing this book is, A. To help all those authors out there who've been scared by social media create their own online platform, and 2. Give them time to actually write.

Novel concept. I know.

Social media doesn't have to be scary. You can use social media effectively (it's really not as scary as some people I know make it out to be) and still have time to write. Social media can be your friend. I'll get you an introduction.

Author, this is Social Media. No, wait come back here. I promise it's not the big, scary, mean, time-sucking monster it looks like. Breathe. Okay, good. Let's try again. Author, this is Social Media. Yes, you can shake hands, it won't bite.

Good job.

Social Media, this is Author. You're going to become good friends.

Any time this all becomes too much, come back to this page, breathe, and read the tips again.

Social media is your friend. It doesn't have to take away from the time you spend doing what you love. Five quality minutes a day is all you really need. Thirty quality minutes spread throughout the day will do wonders.

Coffee Break Social Media Tips

- Be present. Don't post and run. Do take on social media when you will be available to interact should someone respond to you—on any of your platforms. The key is to be social and interactive. Not a robot.

- Use a ten-to-one ratio for marketing yourself or your books. For every ten social interactions you can have one, just one self-promo. People don't like, or buy spam.

- As you get into your platforms and your breaks, you'll learn what you do and don't like to do. DO what you like.

- Don't let social media overwhelm you. If you're jumping between platforms and spending more time on social media than on what you love to do, scale it back. Start back at the beginning and just concentrate on your primary platform. Ease yourself into other platforms when you are good and ready.

The Best Platform is the Next Book

You can spend all day, every day building your platform on social media, but if you don't actually write a book, it won't do you a bit of good. Establishing your platform and using social media is always time spent not writing your book. Without a book, there's nothing for you to establish a platform for. So, get your butt in the chair and write that book. And when you finish that one, write the next one, and the next one. A good quality story will sell you, your brand, and your books better than any website, Facebook post, or tweet.

How This Book Works

In the next chapter, I'll introduce you to the Coffee Break Mentality. It's the key. Social media is there to give you a boost, but it shouldn't take away from your writing time. The coffee break strategies in this book should help you figure out how to be on social media and still have time to write.

You don't have to read every chapter. After you get those key concepts, you can flip through the next few chapters to check out the writer's best social media sites. There's a chapter on your website and blogging, Facebook, Twitter, Pinterest, and Goodreads. For each, there are details on what you need to do once, every once in a while, what to do once you've got your groove on, and what to do on your social media breaks.

There are so many great social media networks these days, that this would be a four-billion-page book if there were a chapter on each of them. Instead, included is a chapter with twelve additional networks with briefs on how to use them. There is also a chapter on Social Media tools, websites, and services to help you get the most out of your social media efforts.

At the end of the book there is an example social media plan, and templates for you to create your own social media plan.

In case I go too techy-fancy-schmancy on you, there is a glossary at the end of the book where you can get simply worded definitions for some of the terms I use.

For example: Platform — noun, a place where you represent yourself and your writing to the world in order to gain more fans. Examples: your website, your Facebook page, your Twitter account, personal appearances, your books, etc.

One Teeny Tiny Final Note

This book will be out of date the moment it's published. It's simply the nature of social media (or today's world, really). This book will have to be updated, and I'll do that, as well as post updates on my website www.coffeebreaksocialmedia.com. But know going in that something in these pages will be wrong, out of date, or simply not exist anymore when you read this. You'll have to do some research on your own sometimes. It's okay. Google will help you.

Let's get started.

The Coffee Break Mentality

The Social Media Coffee Break

What's a social media coffee break, you ask? I'm glad you did.

If you've ever taken a coffee (or tea, or Mountain Dew) break, raise your hand. Good. How long were those breaks? Five minutes? Fifteen? Right. Just enough time to grab a cuppa, let your brain take a break, and then get back to work.

The time you spend on social media should be the same. Five, ten, fifteen minutes, then get back to work. Now, we all know sometimes those coffee breaks turn into an hour around the water cooler, sushi bar, cocktail, or nine holes. They're fun, productive, and you'd be surprised how much business actually gets done on the golf course. And somewhere in your promo plan you may want to schedule some social media social hours. But on a regular basis, you don't need to spend that much time on social media. For realz.

Take Social Media Coffee Breaks (SMCBs) whenever you would normally take a break in your writing time. Health professionals recommend you get up from your computer and clear your head once an hour. Take your SMCBs then, right before or right after you stand up, walk around your office, and stretch.

SMCBs should only take you five to ten minutes at a time. If you complete your work on one platform in three minutes, jump to another for a few minutes. Then get back to work!

"But I don't know what or where to post on social media! There are so many different big scary places on the Internet, I don't even know where to start!" you say. Don't be a whiny baby. You can do this. You're going to do this. You're going to be wildly successful at it and sell a katrillion books and send me a giant check in the mail to say thank you.*

*This is not a guarantee. But feel free to send me a giant check in the mail if you do sell a katrillion books.

So, do you think you can do that? Take a five minute coffee break and share something fun on *gasp* social media?

Quit shaking your head. Yes. You can do it!

Get Up, Up, Up On Your Platform

Most authors' biggest fear is that I'm going to tell them they have to be on fourteen different kinds of social media places (which we will call platforms) and they have to be on them twelve times a day and, and, and . . .

Stop right there. I free you from the fears here and now.

Pick one.

That's right, you heard me. Pick one social media platform (like Facebook, Twitter, etc., ad nauseum) you like and be really good on it. If that is all you ever do. Great. Really.

When you are deciding which platform to make the one, you should choose a place where you enjoy spending time. If you feel guilty because you haven't done your blog or opened Facebook in ages and you really don't want to, then don't choose that as your primary social platform.

If you're too antsy to start with only one platform, that's okay too. But we'll get you going nice and slow. We'll talk about ways to connect across platforms and a teeny bit of automation to help you out with that.

Each chapter profiles one social media platform that could be useful to you, the writer, for building your platform, interacting with fans, and having a little fun. Flip through the chapters and see what strikes your fancy.

Each chapter will list some pros and cons for their specified social media platform. If you're on one or more already, this will help you choose the best one for you to concentrate on.

This will be your primary platform. When you take your social media coffee breaks, this is the first place you go. This is where you gather your people (read: your friends and fans). This is where you post your cheers and your tears (as related to your writing life.) If you only get on social media once a day, a week, a month, this is where you should be.

Once you choose your primary platform, there will be steps to help get you started. Some of the steps are one-time deals, some you should do every once in a while, and then I'll give you ideas of what to actually do on your Social Media Coffee

Breaks. Once you're confident on that platform, there are ideas for the social media barista in you.

You choose what you want to do. After you spend a few Coffee Breaks using your platform you'll discover other things you want to do. Not long after that, you'll feel confident using that platform and you can expand into secondary and tertiary platforms.

There is also a section at the end of the book called Social Media Tools. After you've set up the basics of your chosen platform, check out the tools section. There are websites, apps, and ideas there to make using social media easier.

Once you feel comfortable and confident on that one platform (this could be in a couple of days, weeks, months, years, or maybe never. That's okay. Take your time.), you can start trying out other platforms. Flip through the chapters again and choose another social media site that speaks to you. This will be your secondary platform. If you finish your business on your primary, you can move here to have a little fun on your secondary.

You can eventually even set up tertiary platforms. (Whoo — 25,000-dollar word there!) This is the place that every once in a while you pop on and post something.

Your secondary and tertiary platforms should be linked to your primary platform so you are instantly omnipresent on social media.

Okay, hold up. I know that seemed like a bunch of gobbledy-gook for most of you. Just think of it this way. When you take a coffee break, you automatically chit-chat with the other people around the coffee machine, but maybe you hear or see something so funny you really want to share it with you mom, so you call her on the phone and tell her all about it. Plus, whatever you and your friends and your mom are yucking it up about is so great you print it up and post it on the wall in your office.

Same thing. Just on the Internet.

Even when you've got three or more social media networks, if you use the Coffee Break Mentality, you'll be successful on social media (which means being present and engaging) and still have time to write!

I'll Have My People Contact Your People

In each of the chapters about the different platforms there will also be information on how to find your people. Social media isn't any good if you don't have people to be, you know, social with. I know that you can pay some service to get a bunch of followers or friends or likes, etc. But you don't want to do that. Why? Because those bought friends are just that. They won't be useful to you, they won't pimp your book, and in fact, they will probably ignore you. You need to find people who are genuinely interested in you and your writing. And I don't mean your mom.

People who are in the same industry are a great start. People who write the same kinds of things you do are even better. Writers are readers (or they should be if they want to be any good), so make friends with a whole truckload of writers. Not only will they be so happy when you sell your book or hit the New York Times bestseller list (and be aquamarine with envy), they'll tell other people how excited and jealous they are. These people—your people—will be a great source of information on publishing, writing, books, industry news, and probably some gossip, too.

Do friend, follow, and join groups with people like you.

Don't friend or follow or like every writer you can possibly find just because, you know, they are a writer.

Do friend, follow, and like people, subjects, books, celebrities you like, regardless of the industry.

Don't friend, follow, and like people, places, etc., just because you think it will look good.

Do friend, follow, and like people that follow, friend, and like you IF they are someone you actually like or have an interest in.

But What Do I Say?

You need engaging content to put on social media.

"But, what if I'm not really a very interesting person?"

Hey, you're a writer. That already makes you interesting. Writers are rock stars, dude.

Really, today authors are pretty frickin' cool because they are on social media and people can actually interact with you. People like that because that personal connection they have makes them feel a little bit like a celebrity, too. They go back to work and tell their friends around the water cooler that they talked to the author of that cool amazing book everyone's reading over the weekend.

"But, but... I'm not published yet."

Yet is the key word there, Grasshopper. People will think you're cool just because you are trying to get published. They'll get to say they knew you when. For real.

In each of the chapters on the different platforms I'll give you ideas of some of the best content to put up. But across the board, real life is the bomb, baby. The human condition. Tell the funny story about how you were pulled over for speeding but got out of the ticket by crying/flirting with the hot cop (who is now your husband and inspiration for all your heroes. Or the story about how you wish that would happen to you).

Are you on a diet? There are one point seven zillion people who will commiserate with you, give you advice, and try to get you to eat chocolate cake. Do you love or hate a certain TV show? Me too! Let's tweet about it.

See, even your boring life is actually pretty interesting.

What to Post Tips

Here's my number one tip for what to post on social media. Cats.

Most popular pictures, themes, videos, and blogs on the Internet.

Okay, if you're not into cats, pictures are the most shared items on social media. Picture's worth a thousand words and all that.

Post pictures of the inspirations for your book (and if you don't have any, surf the net and find some, or make them up). Post a rainbow with an inspirational quote. Post the picture you hastily took of the bumper sticker on the car in front of you at Starbucks that said, "What if the hokey pokey is what it's all about?"

That's good stuff and people will respond to it.

Here's my second most popular tip on what to post on social media.

A question.

Not: "How are you today?" But: "Who remembers Gem and the Holograms? Thinking about using them for the theme of my next book. What's your fave 80s cartoon?"

Just writing about that makes me get the "GEM! And the Holograms!" song stuck in my head. And I can talk all about how I got the whole series on DVD for the holidays last year and nobody will watch it with me.

See, boring life, made interesting. (Don't roll your eyes at me.)

Third tip: Links. Did you see the hilarious parody of Downton Abbey that Sesame Street did? Post that all over social media. Did you read a really interesting article on Huffington Post's website about the rise and fall of the bacon nation? Put that on your social media with a blip about why you liked it. People click on links.

Then you can occasionally post about how excited you are that your book is coming out (with the photo of your cover).

Or a contest to win a book, or a myriad of other fun promo about you and your book. Post a link to a great blog post you wrote and ask people if they agree with your ideas. This way you can drive people to your website and books in one out of ten social media posts.

How to Make Friends and Influence People, or How Not to Be an Irritating Spammer

There is only one thing I can say about that.

Be present. Show up. Raise your hand and say "here!" That's all there is to it. When you're on social media, be ON social media. There is a big trend (and all kinds of apps) for automation. Some of which I do like. Some of them are the bane of my werewolf existence. (Get it, wolf's bane? I crack me up.)

I'm not in the never-use-automation camp, but if you use it, it should be used when you are going to be on social media anyway!

Well, why use automation at all? Sometimes you might run across a great blog post you want to share with your friends and followers, but it's not your social media coffee break time. And you know if you get on now it will suck up your whole day. Well, what's a writer to do? Automate that sucker. Yeah, there's an app for that.

You want to promote the blogs of other authors like you and want them to promote your blog? Yeah, there's an app for that too.

I use and love them both. There are a few other ones as well, but I do not use them for posting to my social media platforms when I'm not going to be on them to reply. They just save me time and make my online social media life richer.

The chapter on social media tools will teach you how to use automation to your advantage.

There's more to being present than just posting updates. You need to respond to other people's posts. Show some genuine interest in them and their work. Be social.

Why?

Let me share a little story.

I popped onto Twitter one day and saw someone tweet about not being from America and getting to experience our comfort foods like macaroni and cheese. I did a quick reply and told her I liked mac and cheese way better than meatloaf. We tweeted back and forth a bit more and by the time we were done chatting, a whole three minutes later, this random girl had checked out my twitter profile, clicked on the link to my website, found a recipe on it she liked, linked from my website to my Facebook page, sent me a friend request, and liked my author fan page.

She's going to make my recipe for spicy chocolate pie for her family. And I'll bet you she'll remember that yummy pie and my personal interaction with her when my book comes out.

Did I ask her to go to my website? No. Did I ask her to like my author fan page? No. Did I hard sell her on anything but cheesy childhood comfort food? No. Did I gain a friend and a fan? Yes, I did.

That's why you should be present and engaging when you're on social media. Friends are fans. Fans buy books.

Do post interesting content on your social media platforms about your life, your writing, your cat.

Don't post personal information (like your phone number, address, maiden name, etc.) and be careful about putting up pictures of your kids and grandkids.

Do engage people in a fun and friendly way.

Don't ask them to buy your book every time you talk to them.

Do make friends with the people you meet online.

Don't post and run.

Do post and see who responds. Reply to some other people's posts.

Don't hard sell.

Do share your excitement over your latest release, the sale of your book, the fantastic review you got, and the fact that your mother's dog sitter's best friend's sister liked the sex scene on page 178.

Remember that ten-to-one rule. For every ten interactions you have on social media you can promo yourself one time. And even that may be too much. Don't be a spammer. Be that cool kid everyone wants to hang out with. They'll buy your book.

A Word On Authors Behaving Badly

I wish I didn't have to say this part, but I do. Be careful what you talk about on social media. Politics, religion, money, and strong personal opinions are sketchy ground. If you write inspirational romance, by all means feel free to talk about how your religion has inspired your writing. But if your faith or political party has little to do with the product I'm going to buy from Amazon, leave it off the platform. You are, of course, entitled to your opinions, but is there a segment of the population that might have purchased your book if you hadn't offended them with your rant on the current president, pope, or hot button topic? Think about that before you post anything.

There are a handful of authors whose books I won't ever buy, or don't buy anymore, because of something they have said or done at a personal appearance or online. I'm not trying to scare you. Just remember you are a public personality the second you hit social media, and you need to behave that way.

If you need to rant about your critique partner, your agent, the editor who stupidly passed on your manuscript, or even your family, do it OFFLINE. Rants have no place on your platform.

I'm Not Your Mother

I'm not going to tell anyone they absolutely have to be on any social media platform. I am going to help you choose what will and will not work for you, then help you make it work.

Read on about the different social media platforms available for you. Choose the ones that are right for you. Keep the others in the back of your mind, and, above all, have some fun.

CHAPTER 3

Your Website and Blog: Homebase

Okay, I know I said I wasn't going to make you use any particular kind of social media, and I'm still not going to, but really . . . you need a website.

A website is your home base. It's where your fans and readers can come to find you and you'll always be there.

Can you do this whole social media thing without one? Sure. Do I recommend it? Not so much.

I'm not a computer guru. I can't build you a website. Not even if you pay me. (Well. Maybe if you pay me a lot — or in chocolate) But you, my social media friend, can.

If you want, you can outsource building your website and pay $700 to a nerd in a dark room to build your dot.com empire. Or you can make one yourself for free. There are options for everything in between.

A great place to build a quick and easy website is Wordpress.com. You'll have some small ads on the page, and they'll try to upsell you on all kinds of website goodies, but it's free and lots and lots of authors use it.

The advantages of Wordpress are that you'll have a built-in blog, you can change and update it anytime you want all by yourself, and it's free. You can have your author website up and running in less than an hour.

The disadvantages of using something like Wordpress.com is you won't have your own email address associated with your website, like name@yourname.com. Someday you'll probably want that. Your web address will also have "wordpress" in the URL. For example your address might be something like: www.awesomeauthor.wordpress.com.

Google has a harder time ranking subdomains (which is what you are setting up with Wordpress.com).

If you want your own domain name, for example: www.amydenim.com (see no dot wordpress dot com) in there Wordpress,org can help you there. The dot org part of Wordpress has fee-based services that include buying a dot com domain name. You'll have much higher website rankings and will show up higher in search results with your own domain.

You can always upgrade later to having a hosted site, and you might need to find a web manager/developer to help you. (This is not as scary as it sounds.)But get your blog and website up and running ASAP.

Whether you use Wordpress or not, here is a checklist of items you should consider having on your website:

- **Your website URL** (you know, the web address — www.something.com) with your author name in it. Don't be cutesy. My website is AmyDenim.com. Simple and self-explanatory. If someone Googles Amy Denim, it (should be) the first thing that pops up. If your author name is not available, well, bummer. Try www. Author "Your Name" dot com or www. "Your Name" Author dot com. If all else fails, think about choosing a new pen name.

  It's not the best idea to choose your book title for your website name because you're likely to write more books. This website is all about branding you and your writing. Start off on the right kick-butt foot by creating a website that can expand as your career does.

- **Your name** big and bold across the top of the page. It's you! You're famous (or you will be someday!)

- **Your professional author headshot**. People really, really want to know what you look like. Don't have your mom take the photo (unless she's a professional photographer), and for goodness' sake, don't take a picture of yourself, flexing in the bathroom mirror with your smartphone. If you really can't afford professional headshots, which you can get for as little as $50, try trading something, like say, attribution credit on your website with some up-and-coming photographer who is also starting a business.

- **Your author bio**. Not your whole life's story, but a short-ish bio about who you are, what you write, and maybe why you write. I don't want to hear you live in Upper North Whoville with your genius dog, three evil cats, and a well-trained spouse who loves to garden with you (unless you write books about genius dogs, cats who plot to take over the world, Stepford training, or gardening). There are tons of resources on the Internet for how to write an author bio. Google it.

- **Your contact information**. No, not your home address and phone number, but some sort of contact form where that agent, editor, or fan can get you a message. Wordpress has a great plug-in tool for this.

If you have these five things, you're off to a great start. The rest is all the whipped cream on top of the website sundae.

Here are a few more ideas:

- **A books page**. If you are published, put the covers of those lovely books up front and center. Put up some book blurbs and, most importantly, give me the links to be able to buy them! If you have more than one, it is a really great idea to have those covers scrolling or popping up in sequence so I can see the whole lot of them. And let me know your next release is "coming soon."

- Tip - Consider using an Amazon affiliate account for your own books. (More on that in the tools section).

  If you're not yet published, make this a works-in-progress page. Tell a bit about the projects you're working on. Pretend they are all going to be published books someday soon, and list them just like you would a book. You can even put up some photos to go with it, but avoid fake covers.

- **A news page**. Give your fans an update of what's going on with you and your writing. Is your next book coming out? Great. Let us know when and where to buy it. Are you going to be appearing somewhere? Tell me when and where. I'll be there.

- **A page that is special to you**. This is the page that makes your website cool. If you write cookbooks, put up some recipes. If you write erotica, put up some recipes. (*snort*) If you write about horses, put up some really cool pictures of horses. This page is all about you and your brand. Make this page why your fans think your website is cool and not any other author's website.

- **A sign up for a newsletter**. (There's more on this in the social media tools chapter).

- **Links/buttons** to your social media and accompanying widgets.

- **A blog**. Read more about this next.

Social Media Platform — Blogging

Yes, blogging is most definitely a social media platform. Lots and lots and lots of authors blog. It's a way to warm up your writing fingers. You can stay in touch with your fans. You can run contests. You can post pretty pictures of hot cowboys. (That might just be me.)

Here are some pros and cons to choosing blogging as your social media platform.

Pros

- It's easy for your fans to keep in touch with what's going on with you and your writing.
- You don't have to worry about friending or following anyone else (although, you certainly can and should follow other blogs).
- Every blog post drives traffic directly to your website.
- You control all the content, who sees it, when, and where.
- It's a great way for fans, editors, and agents to get to know you and your writing better.
- You like to write . . . this is writing.

- You don't have to be social quite as often on any other platform. Just the days (and possibly a few days after) you post a blog.

Cons

- You have to come up with all the content.
- It's more words you aren't writing on your current work-in-progress (WIP).
- You have to get people to come and read it; there's no built-in audience.

Is blogging for you?
Check out these steps to get you started.

One Time

Here are some items to sit down and think about before you start blogging. But the good news is you only have to do them once.

- **Come up with a title for your blog**, but be interesting. Musings of an Author probably isn't going to cut it. Make it specific to you and your branding. Be creative. Puns are always good.

- **Make a list of 52 things** you like. It can be anything from books to gardening, from travel to Navy SEALs, and anything in between. If you're struggling to come up with that list, try Googling a couple of your key topics that relate to your branding. There are a couple of great keyword sites where you type in a word or phrase and it will show you related suggestions. I like Ubersuggest.org. Those topic are what you'll blog about this year (and maybe the next!). Add to this list anytime you like.

- **Decide on your blogging schedule**. Don't get scared here. I'm not going to tell you that you must blog every day. Lots of people blog 2–3 times a week. Say Monday, Wednesday, and Friday, or Tuesday and Thursday. I'm an advocate of once a week. Yep. Once a week. That's it. That's all you need. Can't do that? How about once a month? As long as you're consistent.

- **Find out when your people are on** social media and plan to post your blogs just prior to those days. Most people are on social media on the weekends, regardless of industry. Think about posting a blog on Friday nights, so it will be available all weekend.

Every Once in a While

How often you do these coffee break items all depends on how often you've decided you want to blog.

- **Write a blog post**. Look through that list of 52 things you like and pick one. You only have to write a few paragraphs and relate it to you and your writing. If you're published or about to be published, excerpts make great blog posts too.

- **Use lots of keywords in your posts**. Keywords are the buzzwords about you and your writing. Use your name, use the name of your genre, use the title of your book, use your character names, use words that if someone Googled them, they'd find you in your blog posts. Why?
  Google (and all the other search engines) have spiders. Not little black biting bugs, but programs that crawl all over websites and read their content. Then they report back to the big chief bug who updates what people see when they do a search. The more keywords you have that relate to you, the better chance your website and blog will show up. Google et al. ranks websites based on new content and link-backs .The best thing you can do to make sure you rank pretty high is to use lots and lots of keywords every time you write a blog post.

    - Tip — Your blogging site probably has a "tags" section. Put keywords from the blog, your branding, and your books in that tags section too.

- **Your blog title should be specific** and as interesting as a tweet, short and sweet, but informative. NO more than 100 characters (so people can comment on Twitter about it.)

Here are a few examples of Do and Don't blog post titles:

Do: Yay! My Historical Romance Novel EARL LOVE Releases Today. #Party

It's sixty-five characters long. It's specific and uses key words that Google will love. It's exciting. It's not hard selling.

Don't: Go to Amazon and Buy My New Book So I Can Get Busy Writing The Next One #kindle #ebook #buzzbook #INeedMoney

Oi, where to start? It's really long and it's very spammery. Would you read that blog?

Do: Ooh, I Got to Interview Thriller Writer Dirk Darkly #ScaryCover

You tell me, why is this one good?

Don't: INTERVIEW #excerpt #cover #giveaway

And why would I read this? Yeah, that's right, I wouldn't. I don't even know what the blog is about really.

- Tip: You can use hash tags (#) in your blog post title, but don't use more than one—that's just spammy.

• **Use pictures in your blog.** They make your posts more exciting and interesting. But be very careful about how and where you get those pictures. You need to be aware of copyright and infringement. Look for pictures that say they are available for use under Creative Commons licenses. This basically means you can use the picture as long as you attribute the source.

There are several photo sharing sites, like Flickr, that you can search for pictures that people not only don't mind sharing with you, but encourage it. You can also get stock photography, but you usually have to pay for those pictures. They can be affordable, though, and a few stock photo sites have free trials. If you are inclined towards doing your own photography, take some original photos! You can really empower all those pictures by enhancing them with frames, effects and words. Use any photo editing software you may already have on your computer, or check out the Tools section to learn more about my favorite picture tool, PicMonkey.

- Tip — When you post a picture, you can use the caption and the description to attribute the pic. Use the alt text to describe the picture for your blind or visually impaired readers. Yeah, they read blogs too, but instead of reading with their eyes, they read with their ears. Instead of seeing the picture, they get to hear a description of it. If you don't fill in the alt text all they get is "picture" — boring. More inclusive means more readers.

- **Share your blog**. Hit that publish (or schedule button) and then make sure to tell other people you've blogged (this is what other social media platforms are great for). You can post your blog to Facebook or Google+, tweet the link and a fun line or question from the blog, or pin the picture you used in your post to Pinterest with a linkback. Be blog savvy and link your blog to your Goodreads and Amazon pages. That way anytime you post some news or your own bloggy ramblings they will automatically show up on those two platforms.
  You might also tell any writers' loops you are on that you've got an interesting post about, say, hot cowboys, but don't tell your writers' loops about every single blog post you do. That's spammy. (Don't know what writers' loops are? Check out the Other Platforms section on Loops.)

- **Respond to comments** on your blog. If someone takes the time to be social with you, don't be rude. Say hello!

- **Find your people**. You want people to look at and
  read your blog, other bloggers want the same. Make
  friends with other bloggers. Join groups of other
  authors like you that blog. Check out the Triberr
  section. It's a place for bloggers to support each other.
  There are also groups on Facebook and Goodreads with
  bloggers. You'll get some great tips from these people
  on how to blog and what to post about.

  If you have some secondary social media platforms, you
  can tell people about your blog there. Post your blog on
  Facebook or put the link out on Twitter. You can even
  post it (occasionally) to any loops you are on when you
  have something really exciting.

  Email your family and friends and tell them you've
  started or relaunched your blog and ask them if they
  would stop by and read it.

Social Media Barista

You are the master of the blog. Good work. Now let's ramp
it up. Here are some higher-level tasks for you to incorporate
into blogging.

- **Google Analytics** is really useful to tell how much
  traffic is on your blog and from where those visitors are
  coming. It's pretty easy to sign up for an account. Just
  go to http://www.google.com/analytics/ and follow the
  steps.

- **Blog tours** are great traffic drivers to your blog. You schedule guest posts on other people's blogs. Each day you have new and interesting content on some place like a book blog, the blog of another author, or the blog of someone who writes about a topic that is part of your branding, your story, or your genre. Many authors use this as part of their promotion when their books launch. Often you will do giveaways for each of these posts, too. When your tour is done, be sure to offer the other authors a guest slot on your own blog.

  This can be really time consuming, because you have to write something original and interesting for each blog you're on, and then you usually have to respond to comments and follow up on the giveaway. It's hard to tell if it really helps book sales. But if you make sure to put information in your post about your website, you can definitely tell if more traffic is being driven to your blog.

- **A blog hop** is when you and a bunch of other bloggers get together around a theme and a special event. You may schedule to put some theme-related content on your blog on a given day or you all post on the first day of the hop. Each blog drives traffic to the next blog so readers "hop" from blog to blog. Readers are encouraged to go to as many of the blogs on the hop as they can. Again, giveaways are often a big part of these blog hops.

- **Contests** are definitely big traffic generators. People love a free book. Even if you're not published yet you can do giveaways on your blog. Support fellow authors, then when your books come out maybe they'll return the favor. If you are published, these are great to do for your own release. Maybe put a few excerpts on the blog and then culminate in a giveaway.
  - Tip — Don't ever give away something for nothing. Ask people to sign up for your newsletter/mailing list, or join your blog via email. At least ask them a question and have them leave a comment.
  - Tip — Your book is the best giveaway. You don't want people to sign up for your newsletter because you gave away a trip to Hawaii; you want them to sign up because they are interested in your writing. The kind of people who sign up for the prize but aren't actually interested in you aren't worth it.

- **Guests posts** are great traffic generators because not only are your fans excited about some interesting content from an author you like, but their fans will come over to your blog, too. But make sure your guests really are people your readers would like to read. If you write Christian inspirational books, you probably don't want the author of Fifty Shades of Something to guest for you. Even if she is your best friend and critique partner.

Try using you other social media outlets to find people to guest post. A shout out on Facebook, Twitter or your loops asking for guest bloggers is a great way to get some quick results.

- **Polls** are fun for readers and informative for you. Ask questions like, "What should I name my next hero?" or, "Who is your favorite secondary character?" or, "Who from this series would you like to see get a happily ever after?" It makes fans and friends feel like they are involved in your writing process. Blogger and Wordpress both have built in widgets you can use, but you can also use Google polls widget or something similar and get one that will work on your blog.

- **Subscriptions by email and RSS feeds** are ways to get your blog out to your followers and fans. There are plenty of widgets to add to your site so people can subscribe. I don't recommend the widgets that show how many followers you have, like Linky, Networked Blog through Facebook, and others. It takes quite a while to build a decent following, and you don't want to look small-time while you're doing that.
  - Tip — I don't recommend syndicating your blog. It's not worth the risk of losing followers, plus Google won't rate your blog as high if there is duplicate content out there. (If you don't even know what syndication of a blog is, don't worry about it).

- **Don't monetizing your blog.** It puts ads on your blog, and you don't get to choose what they advertise except to say you don't want anything explicit. You're an author, and I know you're poor, but irritating your fans with irrelevant ads isn't the way to make money.

- **Don't clutter your blog with lots of widgets.** Here are my recommended widgets for your blog. For some, I have specific tools I like, but you can always Google the word widget for whatever you need and get plenty of results.
  - An email subscription — Feedburner is a really popular and easy to use.
  - Newsletter sign up — MailChimp is free and easy to use.
  - Twitter feed — The most popular blog sites have one built in.
  - RSS feed — also built in to Wordpress, etc.
  - Content sharing — This allows people to easily share your blog on their social media networks like Facebook, Twitter, Google+, etc. Share This is a popular one.
  - Your social media buttons — If your blog is part of your website, your buttons should be on every single page. They help people connect to you from your home base. This is a good thing.

You can share your blog across platforms pretty easily. If you use blogging as a secondary platform, then definitely share on your primary platform. Many social media websites have an upload your blog feature and most blogging websites have an easy way to share at least on Facebook and Twitter. There's more information in the chapter on Goodreads, but it's pretty easy to link in your blog posts when you set up your author page. Your Amazon author page has a place for social media updates. Link your blog there. For more information on sharing your blog across social media check out the chapter on Triberr.

On your Social Media Coffee Breaks (SMCBs)

If blogging is one of your social media platform here are some ideas of what to do on your coffee breaks.

- **Read and comment on someone else's blog**.

  Bloggers love to see comments, and when you leave a comment you usually have to enter your information, like name and website. If you make interesting comments, other readers of those blogs and the bloggers or blogesses may want to pop over to see your posts too.

  I personally subscribe to blogs I really like and get a lot out of, so I have their posts go straight to my email. Then it's easy to hop on and comment.

  You might choose some book blogs that you like and hope to get a review from someday, to stalk, umm, I mean read regularly, and comment on. If you've been social and supportive of a particular blog, they will be more likely to be supportive of you and your new release later on down the road.

- **Post a Coffee Break Blog**. These are short little blogs that should take you less than ten minutes. They are almost like a Facebook post, but on your blog just so your fans get a quick taste of what you're up to.
  - Coffee Break Blog idea — A music video. Hop on over to YouTube and grab the video for whatever song you jam out to when your writing. Post that and a little blurb about how this song is inspiring your fingers today.

Facebook:
The Most Popular Social
Media Site in the World

Facebook is a social media website that is used more than any other in the whole Universe (assuming aliens don't have an equivalent). More than one-seventh of the world's population is on this social network. Whooo, that's a whole lot of people to hang out with. Can you, or do you even want to, reach out to all of them? Silly. But you do want to find your people.

Here are a few pros and cons for choosing Facebook as one of your social media platforms.

Pros

- There are more users on Facebook than any other social network in the world, so there will be plenty of people to interact with.

- A lot of publishers want you to have a Facebook page. You might as well start now.
- It's easy for people to interact with you on this platform. Because so many people already use it, they don't have to sign up for anything new.
- You are probably already on Facebook, so you know how to use it. This way, you don't have to learn how to use something new and shiny.
- If you're already published and wildly popular, really, Facebook is all you need. Honest. (You don't even need a website if you don't want one if you're a twenty-seven time New York Times bestselling author.)
- Facebook advertising is pretty easy and affordable.

Cons

- Facebook can be a huge time suck. You could spend days on it and never get anything written on your current WIP.
- For most authors, you don't get instant feedback. You might sit there waiting and waiting for someone to like your post or comment.
- It takes a lot of work to get people to "like" your page if you aren't a wildly popular author.
- Facebook is constantly updating and changing. You will need to keep up to date on the best ways to use it.
- If you choose Facebook as one of your platforms, here are some steps to get you going:

One Time

It might take you more than a couple of coffee breaks to get your Facebook page looking and acting the way you want it, but you only have to do it once, so do what you gotta do to make it great.

- **Look at the Facebook profiles and pages of other authors** that you like. You can choose some really successful authors or ones you've heard have good pages. Note one or two things you like about their pages, like the kinds of posts they have, their layout, the interactions, or anything else you could steal as an idea. Use these pages as a model.

- **Set up your author profile and/or fan page** (which is linked to your primary profile) and brand them with the same pictures and profile information you have on your website and other social media platforms.

  You probably already have a personal Facebook profile. I think you need an author Facebook profile with your pen name. This is you, the public personality, the celebrity so you need to be able to interact with readers and fans as that persona.

  I recommend having an author profile (which is where you can interact with people) and an author fan page (where you share news and updates in your writing career.) If you are only using a fan page, it's a little harder to find your people, because you need them to come to you. The best thing you can do is let people know, through your other social media channels and your website, that you have a fan page. Then put great content on it. Check in the SMCB section for content ideas.

If you have a fan page, please use your author name on it. You may have to call it something like "Author Your Name," or even "Fans of Your Name," but make sure your name is on it.

- Tip — When filling out your "About" information on your profile list your Fan Page as where you work. When someone clicks on your place of employment it will link straight to your fan page. Cool.

- **Get a great landing page and profile photo**. This is the first impression for everyone visiting your Facebook page. Make it a good one.

  If you don't think you can do this yourself (there are all kinds of pixel restrictions and stuff), there are plenty of graphic artists who can create this for you. Or, ask a teenager. They're pretty good at it too.

- **Link your pages to your other social media accounts** (like Twitter and LinkedIn), so any time you post on your page it shows up on those platforms too.

Every Once in a While

You'll only have to do this once a week in the beginning, and then maybe once a month-ish after that.

- **Find your people**. If you have a profile page, look for and join groups that do the same thing you do (writers, lovers of your favorite author, readers, etc.).

- **Friend or follow or like five people, businesses, and groups** in your genre. Don't friend every author you find. If you write non-fiction books about airplane engines, it won't do you much good to friend a romance writer (unless said romance writer wants to use you as inspiration for her hero).

- **Invite people to 'like" your fan page**. You can invite people to like your page, but be very very very very very careful with that. It can be really irritating and spammy to be invited to like you. Blech. I suggest inviting a few key people you have a personal relationship with, like your critique group, and then ask them to share your posts to grow some fans.
  If you've been making friends on your author profile you've got some great people to invite to like your page. But don't spread that love like peanut butter on banana pancakes (I'm saying don't go crazy here). Nothing is more irritating than having 527 new FB friends and

invites to like 500 of their pages. You need to have some personal interactions with these new friends before you ask them to support your efforts. Start by asking people you know from your life outside the Internet to like your page and work your way on from there.

Social Media Barista

You are the master of Facebook. Now it's time to use it like you mean it.

- **Customized tabs** are like gold. See that section just under your landing page picture? Just below your profile picture on your fan page? There's a bar there with boxes labeled photos, likes, events, and more. Those boxes are the first thing visitors see after your landing page picture. Use those to your advantage.

  If you have a book trailer or commercial, upload that to this section. You can even upload an excerpt from your book here using Scribd (which is a site that enables you to upload a selection of your book and then link it to your Facebook fan page). Facebook users can't read that unless they like your page. If you want to see an amazing page, check out The Torah Codes page.

  Facebook hasn't made it very easy to customize those tabs. You can log in as a Facebook developer and make an app. But, honestly, that is beyond me. Instead try find a provider to help you. Freebooksy has a really easy

one that allows fans to read an excerpt from your book. Here's the link to learn about it:
http://freebooksy.com/freebooksy-author-marketing-ap

There are already a lot of companies online to add customized tabs. Some are expensive but there are plenty that offer some free or low cost options. Google customized Facebook tabs and you'll get pages of results to choose from.

- **Events** are a great way to garner some attention. A really popular event is an online release party. Your event should be at least two hours long and you should have ways to interact with your friends or fans. Examples include teaser blurbs, guest appearances by your characters, a playlist of songs that go along with your book, posting videos from YouTube that relate to your book, a book scavenger hunt from the new release, trivia questions, and giveaways. The list of things to do is endless. Be creative. Make it fun and exciting.

- **Cross promote** with other authors. When another author you know has an event, like a book release, promote it for them. Post a picture of their book cover, or you getting the book in the mail (or on your e-reader). Put up the links to their books and say how excited you are this book is coming out. Then they promote your releases, too.

You can coordinate and get together with a whole group of authors and do these kind of cross promotions all year if you want.

- **Cross post** with other authors. If you can find another author or group of authors that write in the same genre as you and possibly even the same subgenre, you can attract a lot of interest by cross posting. This can be a one-time event, but a regular Facebook get together will not only garner you attention, but can create a following. The idea is to post pictures, videos, and content tagging your cross posters. Then they respond with a picture, video, or content of their own.

  The best example I've seen of this is a group of romance writers who do Man Wars. They pick a theme, like cowboys, men of the 80s, or whatever is fun, each week and compete to see who can post the best manly picture. They get tons of comments and shares. But the best part is: they gain new fans.

  The first time I encountered the Man Wars I only followed one of the authors, but because it was so much fun and I didn't want to miss any of the posts, I started following the other authors who participated. Great marketing at work there.

- **Fan pages for your series or characters**. If you write a popular series, or a very popular character, you might consider having additional fan pages for them. You'd be surprised how many fictional characters have their own

Facebook pages. But don't do this until you're a multi-published author signing big six- or seven-figure contracts and you can afford to hire an assistant to run them for you.

- **Street team fan page**. Consider starting a fan page for your "street team." Street teams are people who love you and your books so much they want to promote you. And you don't even have to pay them. You might give them a little swag, though. Do some separate research on street teams before you start one. They are a brilliant marketing idea because they are essentially the word-of-mouth marketing you've always heard about but never knew where to find. Facebook is a great place for them to congregate and get nerdy about you and your books.

- **Start a group of your own**. You could start a group for fans of a particular genre or subgenre. How about a group for authors where you brainstorm, critique, discuss promo strategies or anything else your writing hearts' desire.

One of the reasons I like social media so much for authors is because it's free and we're, for the most part, poor. But if you can work it into your marketing budget, there are a few ways to spend your money on Facebook.

- **Promote a post**, and it's pretty cheap. Facebook has all kinds of complicated algorithms about who sees what posts. If you post something by sharing from an outside website, the fewest people see it. If you upload content yourself more people see it. If you really want lots of people to see a particular post like, "Yay! My book releases today and I'm doing a giveaway on my blog."

There's not a lot of information out there on the efficacy of Facebook ads. They aren't very expensive and you can target your audience pretty tightly. This way, the kind of people you want to see your ad are the people on whose pages they pop up.. But frankly, I don't often click on those ads. Do you?

On your Social Media Coffee Breaks (SMCBs)

If Facebook is your primary platform, it should be your first Social Media Coffee Break, and if you only take one SMCB a day, this should be your platform to do it on. If it's your secondary platform, plan on doing some of these things about once or twice a week.

First, a warning. Don't waste your time on Facebook by scrolling through hundreds of posts and liking them. You have to interact. Can you like some posts? Sure. But not if that's all you do. I've got a rule of three for using Facebook.

3 icons

Check out the info bar at the top right-hand side of Facebook. There are three icons. The first looks like two people standing together. These are people who want to be your friend. Go through the requests and approve anyone who looks interesting. Beware of the creepy foreign guy trying to hit on you/sell you into slavery. Friend your people. These are other writers, readers, bloggers, publishers, and editors. But don't forget the people who are interested in the rest of your life, like moms, horse lovers, coffee fiends, etc. Anything you write about probably has some sort of group on Facebook.

The next icon looks like two speech bubbles. These are messages from other people who want to interact with you! Yay! Read those and send messages back appropriately.

Finally, there is a picture of the Earth, and if you're lucky there is a number on it. Those are interaction with your past posts or posts you have liked or commented on. Great! Those are people interacting with you. Go see what they did and interact back.

3 posts

When you're ready to do some posting of your own here are the top three posts people interact with on Facebook. Pictures, videos and questions. So, go out there and post an update. The best posts are something people on FB can interact with. The very best posts ask your friends and followers a question they can respond to. My personal favorite — What's your superpower? You can also ask for their opinions on something or for their help. People love to talk about themselves and give advice. Get people talking.

Remember, cat pictures (or any other pics) are really popular posts. Linking to something your followers will find interesting is also a great idea, but as of right now Facebook doesn't show posts with outside links to as many people as posts where you upload something (like a picture or video).

3 Interactions

Using your author profile, interact on three other people's updates. That doesn't mean just "like" them. The best interaction is a comment. And if it's something your readers and fans would like, share it. You don't have to be the creative one all the time. There are lots and lots of interesting funny people and pages on Facebook. If someone else posts something you relate to or just think is really great, comment and like it, then share the post on your profile or page, too.

Don't get caught up in looking at dozens and hundreds of posts in the timeline. Rule of three — Scroll down only three times to find out what's going on in the newsfeed or you'll be there forever.

Check out what is going on in one of the groups you've joined and make a comment or start a new conversation with a post of your own to the group.

Check out what's happening on one of the pages you've liked and make a comment or share a post.

When you post, tag some of your friends who might want to see your post. Now, wait. I'm not talking about randomly photo tagging a pic of a beautiful sunset and quote with people's names like they are in the picture. I hate that. What I am suggesting is saying something like this:

> Hey @AmyDenim! Saw this photo of a hot cowboy with a cupcake and thought you (and everyone else) might enjoy it. (post the picture.)

Using the @ sign before someone's name should bring up their Facebook name (it will appear in a blue box.) If it doesn't, either you're spelling their name wrong, or you're not friends with them. You can tag multiple people (but don't go crazy, three or four is plenty). They will see the post and perhaps share it with their people, too.

CHAPTER 5

Twitter:
Tweetly-deedly-deet

Twitter is my personal primary platform. I love it, and I'll tell you why. I'm an instant gratification kind of girl and interacting with people on Twitter gives me that hello-how-are-you-right-now connection.

I can tweet somebody and (hopefully) they'll be on and tweet me right back. I can respond to someone's tweet about macaroni and cheese and instantly get a new fan. I can even pitch my book to an agent or editor (in an approved setting, not just throw it out there) and get an instant request.

Twitter is getting a reputation as an author's Mecca. There are many people who know and understand everything writerly there for you to chat with, but more importantly there are readers and book bloggers, agents, and editors.

Here are some pros and cons to using Twitter.

Pros

- It's one of the fastest growing social media platforms. There are already a katrillion people on it and more are joining every day. So you'll have plenty of people to interact with.
- It's short and sweet. You can send out a few a hundred and forty-character tweets and be finished.
- You can interact in real time with people.
- Pretty much every other social media platform has a link to Twitter. You'll see the blue bird button on everything from online articles in the *Times* to *People of Walmart*. It's really easy to share on Twitter.

Cons

- If you're not careful with your time, you could spend years reading the tweet feed. You'll really have to limit yourself.
- It's only 140 characters. If you write 500,000-word novels, it'll be a rough transition for you.
- It's fleeting. You say something and if I wasn't looking, I might miss it.

Twitter Basics

If Twitter is your primary or secondary social media platform, here are a few things to know:

If you choose Twitter as a platform, you have to know about hashtags. They look like this --> # (yeah, that's the pound key to you Americans, and the hash to the rest of the English-speaking world).

Hashtags play a huge part on Twitter. They serve a couple of functions. First, they are a great way to emphasize something you are saying. Twitter doesn't have the option to make your text bolded or italicized. So your only options to accentuate anything you say is either to do all caps, which we all know means you are yelling, or to put a hashtag on it.

Here are a few examples:

Just got the cover art for my latest book. Yay! #LoveIt

Coffee and Oreos are a good cure for a headache, right? #BetterThanAspirin

Hash tags are also for following a trend or a conversation. If you want to do a chat with a group of people on Twitter, you will use a hashtag in all of your tweets. People can click on the hashtag and follow the top tweets or all of the tweets with the same phrase. Be creative because anyone can make up a hashtag. But make sure to keep them short and simple.

Here is a (very short) list of great hashtags for writers.

#writer
#author
#amwriting
#amediting
#writetip

#pubtip

#litchat

#1k1hr

#MyWANA (This one is a reference to Kristin Lamb's wildly popular book, blog, kingdom of We Are Not Alone. You'll find real people who will actually interact with you when you use this hashtag. Use it wisely.

#NaNoWriMo (Every year the Office of Letters and Light runs a month long write-a-palooza. The National Novel Writing Month. 1 months, 50,000 words, 300,000 of your closest writing friends. Put it on your calendar for November, or if you're too busy eating Turkey that month, you can #CampNaNo over the summer.)

There are dozens and thousands more. You'll start discovering them when you start reading some tweets.

Sometimes hashtags are used for events when a group of people all get together on a given day or at a particular time and tweet. These can be a great time to meet some like-minded people and would be a great promo tool. Two of my favorites are #ManCandyMonday and #WineAndWrite. But also watch for people tweeting from conferences and workshops. You could practically attend vicariously through Twitter.

There are also some Twitter events where one person tweets interesting content and everyone else follows along or retweets. A couple of the more famous ones are #AskAgent, #10QueriesIn10Tweets and #EditReport. These are done by agents or editors and can be very useful.

Then hash tags are used for trends. If you are logged in to Twitter, there is a trends area on the homepage. It's on the left below the section that read "Who to follow." Click on any of these and see what people around the world are tweeting about. My personal favorite was when a Big 6 publisher started the #LiteraryTurducken hashtag. Hopefully it will become a Thanksgiving tradition.

Notice that words with hashtags don't have any spaces or punctuation. You can't use dashes or tildes or any other symbol.

The other symbol that is muy importante on Twitter is the @ sign. This is how people talk to one another. Put at @ before someone's twitter handle and then the message.

For example:

> Hey @AmyDenim! Thanks for your help figuring out Twitter. #CouldntDoItWithoutYou

I'll get a notification that you've tweeted something about or for me.

One Time

You'll want to take a little time to set up your Twitterverse so you can get the most out of it.

- **Create your Twitter profile**. You'll have to register and pick a Twitter name or handle. Your handle will begin with @ and then your name with no spaces (and only limited symbols, like _ or -). Your handle should use the shortest and easiest incarnation of your author name. Don't be cutesy. This name is how people communicate with you. If you choose @KittyLover_4869, nobody will know who you are.

If your actual author name is taken, try using an underscore between your first and last name or the word "author" before or after. Try to avoid numbers if you can. Also, keep it short. Twitter limits you to fifteen characters anyway, but every character in your name is one less character anyone can use when they tweet you by name.

See that clockwork cog on the right-hand side of the Twitter website? It's between the search bar and the blue compose-a-tweet box. Click on it and go to settings. This is where you can update your profile, your picture, your header (which is the pretty box behind your picture), your bio, and your connections (like Facebook, etc.).

• **Upload a picture** right away. Nobody follows an egghead, which is what your profile picture looks like until you put up a picture. Use that nice professional headshot you had done for your profile. I don't recommend putting your book cover as your avatar (the picture of you people see online). People want to know they are talking to you, the author, not your weird inanimate book.

- **Fill in your name**, a location (which doesn't have to be real. Do you have a imaginative setting in your books? Why not put that as your locale?) Definitely put in the link to your website. Remember, you're driving people back to your homebase every chance you get (without being spammy) so they can find more information about you, your writing, and your books.

- **Write your bio**. You don't get very much space here — 160 characters — so be succinct. Say what kind of writer you are, or what genre you write, and maybe something about what you'll be tweeting. Represent yourself and your brand. If you are a humor writer, be funny (more people follow funny profiles than anything else aside from celebrities), but if you write dark angsty thrillers, be dark and angsty in your profile.

- **Link accounts**. You may want to hook your Twitter account to Facebook and your other platforms. But be careful here, because everything you tweet will show up there. If you have a strange, convoluted conversation with another author on Twitter, one side of that will show up on your Facebook page and look pretty strange to anyone who follows you.

That's the basics. If you want to stop here, you can. But, if you're feeling creative, go on to the next step of designing your page.

- **The design tab** is the next one down, under profile.

  Twitter has some premade designs that are lovely. If one of the premade designs speaks to you and your brand, by all means, pick it. But if you think they are all yucky, then check out Themelion. (Look just under the premade themes, you'll see it.) You can upload your own images there or choose one of their hundreds of designs. If you upload your own picture, remember that all we get to see is the sides, kind of like margins on the page, so don't go crazy. This is also a great place to display your book covers. Go crazy.

  - Tip - Your header will float behind your picture. This is a great place to put pictures of your book cover or some kind of branding. You should probably avoid putting any words in the header because your bio will be in the middle under your picture.

- **Get a Twitter client application**. This is a program you download to your computer/tablet/smartphone to use Twitter instead of having to go to the website every time. I use Tweetdeck. I would have pulled my hair out long ago without it. There's more information on this social media tool in the chapter called, umm, Social Media Tools.

A couple of Don'ts when you're setting up your Twitter account:

- **Don't protect your tweets**. People will have to request to follow you; each follow request will need approval. Ugh. That's an extra step for both you and the people who want to follow you. Don't make it hard.

Your tweets will only be visible to users you've approved. Other users will not be able to retweet your tweets. Protected tweets will not appear in a Twitter or Google search. Replies you send to people who aren't following you will not be seen by those users (because you have not given them permission to see your tweets). And you cannot share permanent links to your tweets with anyone other than your approved followers.

Why would anyone want to protect their tweets? I recommend it for teenagers and maybe private individuals. You, as an author, are not private. You want people to follow you.

Also, some people say they have problems with spambots. Sounds scary. I'm imagining robots throwing chunks of meaty, slimy spam at me.

A spambot is really someone who follows twitter users for the purpose of, you guessed it, spam. They might reply to you with an ad, or even direct message you. Most spambots are local businesses that search for everyone in their area and follow them in hopes they will follow back. Some are not so nice and innocent. Luckily, Twitter has an easy solution. If you're getting spammed, you can report and block that user. Easy peasy.

- **Don't use a Twitter follower validation service.**
  They say they are protecting you by making sure robots don't follow you. It makes your real potential followers jump through hoops to get access to you. A huge majority of tweeps won't follow anyone who uses these services. I'm anti-Nike on this issue. Just don't do it.

- **Don't use auto-replies.** This is something you can set up using a user client so that if someone follows you a reply tweet or even a direct message is automatically sent out. It may seem like a nice thing for you to say "Hey, Thx for the follow. Check out my book/website/FB page at www.blahblahblah." But it's not.
  It's insincere and spammy. I know it's not actually you tweeting me. Remember, we're on Twitter to actually interact with people.

Every Once in a While

Do these about once a week or so.

- **Find your people.** Check out the profile of someone you like, admire, or an author who writes in the same genre as you. See who follows them and who they are following. This is a great place to find new people. Follow ten to fifty or so of their followers or the people they follow that are interesting to you. The newer ones will be at the top of the list. Follow them first because they will have most recently followed, or have been followed, so are likely to be more active.

- **Keep the keepers**. Go through the people you follow and see who's been active on social media, who's tweeted interesting content, and who has followed you back. These are your keepers. Anyone who hasn't tweeted in over a couple of months isn't being social and isn't useful to you. Go ahead, unfollow them. (They won't even know you did it. So don't be afraid of hurting their feelings.)

Social Media Barista

You are a tweeting machine. Now it's time to get fancypants.

- **Create your own hashtag**. It's time. It can be a one-time thing or even better, something that you can use over and over that's branded to you and when people see it they'll think — oh, it's that one author I like so much. Your hashtag should be short but self-explanatory. Try the name of your book or your character, even the name of your fictional town would work. Then tweet using it.

■ Tip — You can register your hashtag if it's something unique. Check out www.twubs.com

- **Host a Twitter event.** This is something scheduled, where you and other tweeps get together and tweet about things. If you can add pictures and humor to these events, even better. You'll want to use a hashtag you create for the event and make sure you and your followers use it for any tweets relating to it, even replies.

- **Have a Twitter party.** It's just like a Twitter event, but you do it one time or a few if they are leading up to a release. Remember to invite people and put some interesting content up during the party. Use a hashtag that is unique so people can follow along.

- **Do an author chat** on Twitter. Just like the parties and events, you should schedule it ahead of time and invite people, then use a unique hashtag. Ask some fans or friends ahead of time to ask you questions and get the ball rolling. Nobody wants to be the first to speak up, but after you warm the "room" up and other people start seeing the tweets with the hashtags, more Tweeps will join in.

On Your Social Media Coffee Breaks

Got a couple minutes to pop online? Here's what you can do on your Twitter Coffee Breaks.

- **Check to see if anyone has interacted with you**.

  On the Twitter website, across the top on the left there is a button that says @connect. Click on that first thing when you log in. This is where you can see who has followed you and who's tweeted you. Reply to everyone who tweets you! DON'T just say thanks. DO comment on what they said.

  If you only have a few mentions, or none, retweet a few tweets you like and that your followers would like. If you can, comment on those retweets. Examples

  So useful for #novelwriters --> (the original tweet)

  Loved this! --> (the original tweet)

  This is sooooo me! --> (the original tweet) etc.

  I like using arrows in tweets to draw attention to things. You don't need them, but they're fun.

- **Interact with someone**. Anyone! Reply to anyone in the stream to get a short conversation going. You may have to try a few people to find someone else who is actually online.

- **Follow five people**. Twitter is a follow-back culture. Most people will follow you if you follow them. A great place to find like-minded people is on the hashtags you like. I'm always following people who are on #1k1hr so I have plenty of buddies to write with.

CHAPTER 6

Pinterest:
The Virtual Corkboard

You know how it used to be in the prehistoric times (read: the 90s) and you saw a funny comic, an inspirational quote, or got a picture of a hot guy from Teen Beat magazine? What did you do with them? You put them on your wall or on a bulletin board in your office.

That's pretty much what Pinterest is, but on the Internet. When you sign up, you get a bunch of virtual bulletin boards on which you can virtually pin things.

Why would a writer want to do that? Remember, a picture is worth a thousand words. Plus, Pinterest is currently the fastest growing social media website, like, ever. And here's the part that has businesses excited. The referral traffic percentages (which means people click and go to the seller's website and possibly buy something) rate from Pinterest is higher than YouTube, Google+, and LinkedIn combined! Also, the people who click through from Pinterest tend to spend a whole lot more money than from other social media sites.

Now, that won't last forever. Pretty soon people will get wise to cheesy marketing techniques from big brands and they will flee, ruining it for the rest of us. (Just like what happened to MySpace years ago.) Get using it while you can.

Before you read the Pros and Cons, you should know that I don't recommend Pinterest as your primary platform. But I love it for a secondary or tertiary platform. It's all good to flock to Pinterest and spend all your marketing efforts there if you're a wealthy conglomerate of window coverings and you're hawking your products by putting pretty pictures for Pinners to enjoy or pin to their board of their dream homes, and then click through and buy. That's not us. It's hard to be social on Pinterest. It's possible, but it would take more time that I think you want to put into social media. Check out the Cons for more information.

Pros

- See that referral traffic percentage from above.
- If you happen to be a romance, chick lit, or women's fiction writer, Pinners are exactly your demographic. If you're not into the whole happily-ever-after genre, guess what? Those same people are also the main buyers of books for a majority of households. Who are these golden magical consumers? Women aged 26–44 (who also happen to have an average annual household income of $100,000). You want to market to these women. They are the ones who buy your books.

- There's not a whole lot of personal interaction on Pinterest, so if you are a social media recluse you can pin and run. You don't actually have to talk with anyone.
- Fans love to see your inspirations. It gives them a glimpse into the mind of you, the celebrity.

Cons

- There isn't a whole lot of social interaction on Pinterest, so if you want to actually talk to someone and develop a relationship it's a little bit harder.
- Huge, huge, huge time suck if you aren't careful. I've spent hours, days, whole weeks looking at all the funny or cool pictures people post.
- There's a tiny bit of worry about the legalities of posting pictures. You have to be careful where you get your posts and if you have the right to share them with the online world.

    My best advice for this is to create your own content. Use pictures from ads (because, hey, more buzz about that advertising campaign is always welcome) and your own. Check out the section on Tools to see how PicMonkey can help you make your pictures awesome. Your own pictures can link back to your website and that will drive more traffic your way. That's good.

- If you find something really cool you want to pin, make sure it links back to the original. Even that may not be good enough if the pic doesn't allow for Creative Commons rights.

One Time

Take a couple o 'coffee breaks to get your new virtual wall personalized and optimized.

- **Sign up for a Pinterest account** and fill in your profile. If you're very serious about using this site to promote yourself, consider a business account. One advantage of a business account is the analytics.

- **Personalize your boards**. The site starts you with some generic boards, but you need to personalize these. Everybody has the For the Home board, but nobody else will have the For (insert character's name here) board. Be creative with your board names and relate them to you and your brand.

  Remember, people want to feel connected to you, the celebrity, and with Pinterest they feel like they get to see inside your head. I suggest some boards with pictures that are meaningful to your book. I have a board for each of my works in progress (WIPs) that is called "title of the book" muses. Then I put pictures of people I think look like or inspire my hero and heroine. You can put pictures of the setting, gadgets, and cars and toys they have. Anything that gives insight into the book. I've also heard from an author that used her Pinterest board to give the inspiration to her art department when they were working on her cover. Smart.

- **Add the Pin It button** to your bookmarks bar or your toolbar. Google Chrome has an Add-in to do this and it will make pinning a whole lot easier.

- **Link your Pinterest account**. Because Pinterest is a great secondary or tertiary platform, you may want to hook it up to Facebook (if you're using it). In your settings, you can select to automatically publish to your Facebook Timeline. Anytime you put a picture there, it will also go to your Facebook page. You can also add your Twitter account information and anytime you pin it will ask if you want to tweet your pin (and you do want to if you're using that platform.)

Every Once in a While

Pinterest isn't as time intensive as some of the others, so you won't have to take a lot of time to do these every week.

- **Find your people**. Use the search bar and type in some keywords for people you're looking for. Try your genre, e.g. Mystery, Romance, Business, etc. Or try more generic things like books, readers, writers, etc. Like most social media sites, you'll follow people and they'll follow you. The more people that follow you, the more people see your pins.

If you're using a Facebook profile page, you can use the Find Friends button in Pinterest to follow all your friends who are already on Pinterest. Don't invite a bunch of people from Facebook to Pinterest, that's spammy. You can recommend it to some of your close personal friends (and then recommend they get this book and read how to use SMCBs too.)

- **Follow a few pinners or their boards that have content you like**. It's a follow-back culture at Pinterest, so they will likely follow you back. Repin from them and they'll be even more likely to follow you back.

Social Media Barista

Feeling social media savvy?

- **Try a Pinterest contest**. Contest rules and guidelines for contests are waaaaaaaaay simpler on Pinterest than on Facebook. (You have to practically give away all of your future children to run a contest there.) But Pinterest contests are generally pretty easy and can be a lot of fun for Pinners.

  The basics are: Ask people to follow you or one of your boards and then they do something like create their own board based off your contest or something of the like. The key to a Pinterest contest is to have the pinners use hashtags because, similar to Twitter, they are used for searches. And, of course, you have to give something away. Perhaps your new book?

If you really want to do a Pinterest contest, Google it and check out some of the articles out there on good tips and ideas for contests. Pinterest also has a contests page that you might want to be on and will give higher priority to contests entered into their case study.

- **Have a public/collaboration board.** When you create a new board in Pinterest, you have a "Who can pin?" option. You can add members either by their Pinterest member name or their email address. If you start typing a member name in the text box, Pinterest automatically populates a list of possible matches, and you can select the right person from the list. Then just click the Add button next to the name.

  Don't invite people willy-nilly. That's spammy. Do ask people on your primary social media if they'd like to join your pin-a-palooza and add the people who are excited about it.

- **Pin from your website/blog.** Remember, every picture has a link for where it came from, so if you can post something that is on your own website (maybe in a blog post?) then it drives traffic back to you. And if other people pin an image from you it adds all kind of legitimacy in Google's eyes to your website by having external link-backs. Sweet.

- **Add the Pin It button** to the pictures and images on your website/blog. If you're creating images on your website or you have your book covers on there, add the Pin It button to those.

On your Social Media Coffee Breaks

I like these ones because you can find stuff to pin anywhere you are on the internet, not just on this platform.

- **Pin a picture**. Yep, that's it. If you're on Twitter, click the box to tweet it too.
  But what to pin?

- **Get some content on your boards**. Start pinning and repinning pictures. Pin pictures you already have or have found. The majority of pictures on Pinterest are repins. Use that search bar at the top of the page to search for something you're interested in. Check out the results and repin pictures other Pinterest users/Pinners have on their boards.

- **Create new content**. The best thing you can do here is bring something new to the board. Most pinners are re-pinners. So why not give them something new to re-pin?

Here are my favorite new content items for you to create and pin:

- **Teaser** — If you have something new or interesting on your website (say, your new book or your latest blog post) you want to promo, create a teaser. Find a picture that speaks to your content and put words across it like your logline or a quote. Think magazine ad. So it has to be cute, funny, unique, and/or clever to get people re-pinning.

- **Helper** — Share your knowledge with the world by creating something that can help them in some way. Examples are checklists and tutorials.
Checklist ideas: Do you have a conference you go to every year? How about a checklist to get the most out of the conference? Or maybe you have a huge series or several series. How about a readers' checklist/guide to your books? Tutorial ideas: What do you know how to do? I'll bet you did a bunch of research somewhere along the way for one of your books. Did you learn anything that you could teach through pictures? Maybe you know how to dress a Regency lady from the knickers up. Do it with a paper doll and take pictures along the way. Maybe you know how to slay a zombie in three quick and easy steps. I'd pretty much pay to see that tutorial.

- **Video** — Yeah, yeah. They aren't technically pictures, but you can certainly pin them too. And if you're creating videos for YouTube or Vine, you can do double duty there.

Don't have time to create something new to pin?

- **Look for the Pin It button all over the Internet**. When you see a picture somewhere on the Internet (except Facebook — right now there is no pinning directly from Facebook) first, check to see if there is a Pin It button. If so, have at it. If not, check to see if you think you can legally pin a picture from this website. A big no-no is the pictures that bear that copyright symbol. Run far, far away from those. Then use your Pin It button and choose the picture you like. Add a caption and a hashtag, which will make it pop up in searches on Pinterest (and works great when you post to Twitter, too), choose which board you want to put it on (or start a new board), and pin it.

- **Re-pin**. When you first log in to Pinterest you'll see the news feed. It's a bunch of pictures they think you'll like based on what kind of boards you have. Today, based on my boards, I saw chocolate chip brownie bombs (totally repinned and am making them this weekend), some Christian Louboutin can't-walk-in-but-they're-so-pretty shoes, a board called Swoon Worthy Men, and a whole lot more. I repinned my favorites. Check out your feed and re-pin something.

CHAPTER 7

Goodreads:
The Virtual Book Club

Do you like to read books? Goodness, I hope so. Then you'll like Goodreads. It's just a great big website full of other people who like to read and talk about books. There are other social media sites for books out there, like Shelfari, BookLikes, and LibraryThing, but Goodreads is twice as large as those three combined. There are tens of thousands of reviews written every day on this site. Readers, librarians, book bloggers, publishers, teachers, and authors are the kind of people who are active here. These are your people!

This one isn't too complicated. If you're a published author, you're probably already on it anyway.

Pros

- It's a pretty captive audience. The whole reason people are on Goodreads in the first place is because they like to read. Yay!

- Any marketing, promo, and platform building efforts you do here is directly to your target audience. Readers. You don't have to worry that you are wasting your time on thousands of people who don't read and buy books.

- If you're already published, it doesn't have to be very labor or time-intensive. You can do most of your interactions through automation (uploading your blog) and it doesn't look bad, like on other social media sites.

- Goodreads makes it really easy to do promos on their site, with giveaways and chats.

- It's pretty fun for us book-nerd types to get to keep track of all the books we've read and discuss them with other nerdy book-types.

- The Goodreads newsletter has approximately four million subscribers.

- Goodreads reviews appear on lots of library catalogs and places that sell books online.

Cons

- If you're not already published, it can be a little more of a time suck.

- You can get overwhelmed really easily if you get caught up in all the groups.

- Spammy authors. There are a lot of them on Goodreads and I really wish they would quit trying to be my friend and push their book on me. Do I think you should join Goodreads? Yes. Do I think you should friend everyone you possibly can and then send them lots of messages asking them to buy, like, tell your friends about, review, and sleep with your book? Umm . . . no. In fact, I won't friend someone who has more friends than books.

One Time

Before you do a whole lot on Goodreads I want you to get educated. So some of these one-time items are especially for that. Other to-dos directly affect your author or profile page. I have to say that setting up Goodreads was some of the most fun I've had online because it's all about books. I think you'll like it too.

- **Check out the author's program page**. Click through the slideshow. If you're a published author, claim your author page. Right now. Really. Go. Don't read any further until you've done that. Then come back and learn more. Go. Get.

- **Get your books are listed on your author page** (and make sure all the books listed are actually yours).

- **Create a series**. If your book is part of a series, make sure you have the series list, even if only the first book is out. A Goodreads librarian will need to help you do this.

- **Link your other social media**. If you're using Facebook, add a Goodreads tab to your fan page so you can show off your books.

- **Set up your profile** whether you're published or not. Do all the steps including your picture and bio.

- **Add some books**. Books you've read, books you want to read, and books you're currently reading. Don't go crazy, you can add more every once in a while. You want to do this because people are really nosy and want to know what you read. This is especially fun for fans to see what you're reading. You may want to only rate books you like (4 or 5 stars) because you don't want to alienate one of your readers by saying you didn't like the books she wrote.

  You may not want to do any reviews. There are rumors that published authors often have their reviews removed anyway, for strange and partially unknown reasons about conflicts of interest or something.

- **Find a Goodreads librarian**. There are tons of things you can't do by yourself on Goodreads, so you want to find someone to help you. I found mine by using my other social media sites and just posting a "Help me, who is a Goodreads librarian?" post on Facebook and Twitter.

Every Once in a While

Do these items once a week to once a month.

If you're unpublished:

- **Join a Goodreads group**. These are sort of like online book clubs. Goodreads users start them and either the moderator or the group chooses what to read. If you are active in a group, contribute to the conversations, and everyone gets to know you, then someday when your book comes out, you can ask the moderators if they can add it to the reading list. They will be much more likely to if they feel like you've become their online friend.

  You can announce to the group how excited you are to be published in this, your favorite genre. Be really careful about not being spammy here. One announcement that is a hip-hip-hooray kind of thing, not a hey-everybody-buy-my-book thing, will be plenty. Choose a group that reads (or role-plays, which is a really interesting phenomenon on Goodreads) your genre.

Now look through the ideas for published authors (next) because you may be able to use some of them, too.

If you're published:

- **Add a preview of your book**. Yeah, people can read a sample of your work right there on Goodreads.

- **Add a quote from your book**. Start with the Explore tab and look for the quotes button. It's pretty easy to do if you just follow the prompts. There are also some great tutorials you can find on Google on how to do this.

- **Add videos** of interviews, book trailers, and such to your page. If you've ever done a recorded interview, this is a great thing to put on Goodreads. Many authors have jumped on the book trailer wagon; upload those too!

- **Create a list** of your favorite books and recent reads to share with your fans. Remember you're a celebrity (really, you are!) and people want to know about your personal life. This is a great way to let people into your world without getting creepy stalkers and p-p-p-paparazzi.

- **Add content from Goodreads to your website**. Add some of your great reviews and some quotes from Goodreads on you're my Books page on your website. It makes you look cool and legit if people are talking about you on another website. Don't quote from these. Goodreads has a really easy to use widget and it will look nice and official.
  In fact, they have more widgets than a one-armed paper hanger in a widget factory. Check out their help page or Google Goodreads widgets.

Now read through the unpublished author's section and try some of those ideas too.

Social Media Barista

You're the master of the Goodreads world, so now it's time to conquer the whole universe. There are some kick-butt ways to promote you and your books on Goodreads, and the smart marketing department over there makes it all pretty easy to do.

- **Start a Goodreads group** of your own. If there just aren't any other groups that support your kind of writing, start one of your own. If you write paranormal romance, don't bother. There are many groups who love to read and talk about that genre, and they have a truckload of members. But if your write foodie horror (which I would totally read, by the way) then go for it. Start that group up and recommend some reads other than just your book.

- **Do a Goodreads chat**, aka create a featured author group. Unless you're a pretty big name, like say Nora Roberts or Steven King, you won't get to do the Goodreads live chats. You can still do a chat with all your fans (and maybe make some new ones) with a Q & A.

  You set up a group, call it something, hopefully more clever than Q&A with Author, advertise through other social media channels and your website about when and where you have having a chat, and then be there. Goodreads recommends doing it on just one day. People can post questions and you respond.

  The advantage of a chat on Goodreads in a group is that the questions and answers stay up for anyone else to read at a later date. I also recommend asking a couple of your friends/authors you know/really amazing fans to join the chat and get things started. Some people are shy even online and don't want to be the first person to ask you, the big famous author, a question. Afterwards you can add the link to your website. Some really great author chats are featured in the Goodreads newsletter every month.

- **Goodreads giveaways** are really great for getting you and your book noticed. Goodreads says an average of around 700 people sign up for the average giveaway and a big percentage of those people add your book to their To-Be-Read shelves. About half of the winners tend to post a review afterward as well.

  Unfortunately, they haven't figured out a way to host e-book giveaways yet, so this one is only a go if you have a book in print. Check out the author program on how to set up your giveaway and the best times to do them. Goodreads recommends a couple months prior to your release. This can really help boost your pre-release sales.

- **Listopia**. Get your book on a few of the listopia lists. Explore the categories and lists and find a few that your book fits into well. Add your book to the list and don't forget to vote. Use your other social media sites to let people know your book is on a list and suggest that it might be fun for them to peruse the list and vote. You can also start a list of your own that other people can add books to.

- **Use Goodreads self-serve advertising**. They've made it incredibly easy to put an ad on their site. Follow the instructions to create your ad, target your market, and select a budget and dates to run it. You put in a bid for each click, which averages $0.50. The higher your bid the more likely your ad will be shown first on the homepage.

The great thing about the self-serve ads is being able to choose a daily limit for your budget. You know you won't spend more than X dollars a day. You also know you're targeting your demographic when you choose who to target. You can even list other authors whose work compares to your title. When users are viewing books by those authors your ad will be on that page.

You can also combine your ad with a giveaway to drive even more readers to your book's page on Goodreads. Think about running an ad for about two weeks, one before and after your release. You can run a campaign for about $100 at $7.00 a day with up to fourteen clicks at $0.50 each. Play around with the numbers and see what works for your budget.

- **Volunteer to host an activity** for one of your groups.

  Most of the groups (that you want to join) are a lot like an online book club. Book clubs have activities like reading challenges, book swaps, bookmark swaps, choose my next read, and many more. The moderators for groups are often super busy running all these activities. You can reach out to the moderators and offer to be in charge of an activity, or even start a new activity. They'll probably love you for it. Make sure you're a good host and are very active when running that activity. You're getting your name in front of some really enthusiastic readers. You don't want to slack.

- **Become a Goodreads librarian**. Once you have 50 books in your profile (not books you've written and published, but books you've read, want to read, or are currently reading), you can apply to be a librarian. You can fix problems with books yourself, create series, and all kinds of fun stuff. Librarians are all about making sure Goodreads stays organized. Other people may also contact you to help them make their own author pages accurate.

On your Social Media Coffee Breaks

You get to play books!

- **Add a few books to your lists**. Something you're reading, something you want to read, and something you've read. Listopia is a great place to find books you like if you're stuck. You can even add some of your own books to a Listopia list or start one of your own.

- **Add a comment** to one of the threads in one of the groups you're in. The point of this one is to actually be social. See what other people are talking about in your groups and add to the conversation. Most of the time it's book talk about what you're reading, recommendations, or what you should read next. A really fun way to interact is to ask other people to vote on what you will read next.

- **Add a friend**. If you're unpublished, try adding a couple people in one of your groups. Target people who will be readers of your books someday. Don't send out friend requests to everyone and their book blog. Be selective. Also, don't feel obligated to accept friend requests of people who aren't in your target audience either.

  Here's a really important part of using Goodreads. Have more books than friends. Yeah, Goodreads is about being social about books. But I absolutely will not friend someone who has more friends than books because he or she is probably an author who is going to spam me later with requests to read, review, and buy their book. People are not on Goodreads to be marketed to, they are there to track the books they read and talk about them.

CHAPTER 8

Other Platforms: Claiming Your Virtual Real Estate

I'm pretty sure a new social media site pops up at least every week these days. And of course, they are always the next big thing. In the previous chapters I've detailed the ones I personally think are most useful to authors, but none of them will work for you if you aren't comfortable using them and interacting with people. Maybe you're on one of these other popular networks. If you are, they can be a great place to establish your platform as well. Maybe you just want more options. Well, here they are.

Some of these social networks aren't cut out to be a primary or even a secondary platform, but are fun in order to add some spice to your updates and posts. I'll note the platforms that are good additions to your top platforms, but shouldn't replace them.

Most of us have at least a couple of social media accounts, and if you didn't before you read this book, you probably do now. If you've embraced the Coffee Break mentality, you've chosen your few accounts and you're sticking to 'em. Good job. But it might be a good idea to claim your virtual real estate in more places than you ever plan to actually use. Why? I have no doubt you're going to be rich and famous someday and you don't want a crazed fan tumbling, tweeting, and tubing under your name. Also, you should grab your name on a bunch of social media sites in case you want to use them yourself someday.

Don't freak out here. I'm not saying you need a million social media accounts. Just a few. It's okay for you to sign up for them and never use them. Just be sure to write down your usernames and passwords somewhere.

Amazon

This isn't exactly another social media network, but it is vital for writers to have a presence here. You may love your local brick and mortar bookstore and hate the giant book beast, but if you actually want to sell books, then Amazon is the number-one place to be.

Besides your author page, Amazon also has message boards. Joining, reading, and commenting here can really help you keep your pulse on what's going on in the Amazon community.

Plus, don't forget about the reviews. We all need good reviews on Amazon. It's one of the best word-of-mouth promotions out there. But don't ever, ever, ever, ever fake or pay for reviews. Sure, you should ask your friends and family to review your book, and absolutely you should provide your book to people for free in exchange for a fair review. Just know that most people skip the first five or six reviews knowing that it's your friends and family. There is nothing like that first five-star review you get from someone you don't even know. When you get it (and I know you will!), print that sucka out and frame it.

Pros

- Your author page links up well to lots of other platforms and could possibly be the only place your readers get to know you.
- Amazon actually wants you to sell books, so they try really hard to make it easy for you to use.

- This is where the majority of book buyers are buying their books. You buy some of yours there too, don't you? (And if you don't, do you do it for some ideological reason while knowing that zillions of other people buy their books there?)

Cons

- You could get obsessed with checking your rankings and sales, and spend all your time on Amazon obsessing over all the analytics, while you should be writing your next book.

One Time

- **Claim your author page** and optimize it. Get a good bio on there. There's information about bios in the website section near the beginning of the book. Keep that bio short, sweet, and clever. Don't go on and on about your masters in creative writing from Hoity Toity U. If you're writing fiction, nobody cares. If you're writing non-fiction, it had better be relevant if you're going to mention it. Make sure there is a link to your website and your other social media accounts there (but don't go crazy, just use your primary and secondary platforms).
  - Tip — Did you know you can claim your author page for Amazon in other countries too? Amazon expands to other counties all the time. Right now

you can grab you page in The UK, Germany, France and Japan.

- **Add pictures** (check out the Pinterest section on Teasers for ideas) and videos. A personal picture of you writing, reading, or meeting fans is great, but this is a great place to put up pictures that relate to your book, almost (exactly like) a magazine ad.

Every Once in a While

Go to the forums and message boards relevant to your genre and see what people have to say. Interact in a non-authory, non-spammy way. This is not the place to plug your book. It's a place to get to know what readers are thinking.

Social Media Barista

- **Link your blog, Twitter, and Facebook** feeds so fans or potential fans checking you out know you're a real, live person.
- **Contact Amazon super reviewers** to see if they are interested in your book and would like to review it. They are super reviewers because that's exactly what they like to do. Read and review.

On your Social Media Coffee Breaks

- **Check your rankings** and your sales if you have a published book on Amazon. But limit this to your SMCBs. And don't start taking a lot of additional breaks just because you've got a book out and want to check the ranks.

- **Review a book**. The best thing you can do for another author is to leave a great review for them. Don't lie, be honest, but it doesn't do you or any other author any good to leave a one-star review. Leave that up to the meanie heads.

  There has been talk that Amazon removes reviews from other authors, especially if you write in the same genre. Something about competition. But there are an awful lot of books and lots of reviews. The best way around this is to review books outside of your genre.

  However, if you happen to be a big ole you, like say Nora Roberts, Stephen King, or Bill Clinton, well, first, let me say thank you for reading my book, and second, if you've read a book you really enjoyed, you should think about offering an unsolicited book quote. You'll make that newer author's millennium.

Google+

Google is not so slowly and surely taking over the world, along with Amazon. It benefits you to use their social media network to build your platform. It's especially good for men. Not sure why, but the demographic on this site is more male than female. So if you write the opposite of chick-lit, get your butt onto Google+. Don't believe me? Check out Guy Kawasaki, the author of books like APE: Author, Publisher, Entrepreneur and What the Plus? He's a Google+ god.

Pros

- Google loves to give preferential treatment to their own social network. Google+ content shows up higher in searches and so it's a great place to get noticed.
- The circles are a good way to keep your audience organized and target your platform outreach.

Cons

Google swore they were going to be bigger than Facebook. Not so much. They are growing, but there aren't quite the cool kids on the block yet. They're more like the nerdy kid who will someday come back for a class reunion and have more power, influence, and money than Bill Gates. But for now, they're just lusting after the prom queen.

One Time

- **Set up a Google+ account.** Remember this is Google's baby so, yeah, you want stuff in your Google+ profile that will help readers and fans find you. Include information relevant to the books you write so that if someone was searching for a similar kind of book, they'll find you.

  For example my Google+ profile has key words like: Contemporary Romance, Cowboys, Cupcakes, and more. Just a glance by a reader should tell them if I'm the kind of author they might like to read. Your profile should too. Also make sure to add links to your website, other social media platforms, and contributors to you blog.

- **Add some people to your circles.** There's a tool to search your other social media and email contacts to find people you already know and add them. But, you should also do some searching using keywords for your books, your brand, etc. to find like people.

  It's a great idea to organize your circles by target audience. For example, you might have a circle for authors, readers, fans, book bloggers, etc. and then when you post an update you can target who will see it. Be sure to use keywords for search engine optimization.

Every Once in a While

- **Join some communities**. There's a toolbar on the left-hand side of your Google+ page and one of the buttons is labeled "communities." Click on that and check out what's popular. You should also search for writers, readers, and your genre and join a few of those groups too. Don't go crazy. Join ones that are active, but not too many, because you need to be active in those groups to connect with people and use this platform effectively.

- **Start posting interesting content**. If you blog, this is a great place to get some engagement. Most of the same things you might do on Facebook you can do on Google+, so throw up some pictures of cute cats, ask some questions, and engage with other plusers. If you're going to make Google+ your primary or secondary platform, read the Facebook chapter and do any and all of those ideas.

Social Media Barista

Are you a Google-meister?

- **Sign up for Google+ authorship**. I wish this meant that Google helped you be an author of books, but it doesn't. It's an easy way to connect content you create on your website (or other websites you create content on for that matter) to Google+. When someone Googles you links for articles and posts you've written (on your website or anywhere else your headshot and info will appear along with the links in the search results. Pretty cool, huh?

- **Add a link to your Google+ profile** on your blog posts, and probably a +1 button too.

- **Have a Google Hangout**. There are tons of fun ways to use this application. It's essentially an online meeting tool, but it has so many great features that are useful for connecting and promoting.

  Google Hangouts can be a great forum for a critique group! You could have an intimate chat with up to nine fans. Have a contest on your website or blog (or any other social media platform) for readers to win the opportunity to chat with you in a hangout. You can live stream Google Hangouts on Google+ and your own website. These live Hangouts are also recorded via YouTube, so you can have the hangout on your website or blog for new fans and readers to experience at a later date.

On your Social Media Coffee Breaks

Post an update or comment on other people's updates. Try a Google+ event. See the Facebook chapter for more ideas.

LinkedIn

LinkedIn is like Facebook for professionals. There are no games, no drunken frat party pictures, or cats saying funny things. This social media network is for grown-ups! Or anyone looking to make professional connections.

Pros

- You don't have to post funny pictures to engage with people here, in fact, LinkedIners probably won't play with you if you do.
- There are a lot of really interesting and active groups for authors here that discuss everything from craft to marketing. You can get a lot of great tips and ideas by joining in the discussions in those groups.
- This is a great place to advance any other income streams you have besides your books, like speaking engagements, workshops, or other professional services.

Cons

- You're not supposed to Link with anyone you don't already know professionally, so it can be hard to grow your network if you're just starting out and/or if you're using a pen name. You'll need to make those connections outside of LinkedIn. You will be able to add a few connections by being very active in groups, but that's really not enough for this social media platform to be effective.

- This is not a great place to attract readers. However, authors are also readers, so if you make some good friends here, some of them will probably buy your book.
- There's a lot of promotion going on in the author groups on LinkedIn. I personally am not going to buy the book of everyone in my groups, so it's not effective marketing at all. I will buy books by the authors I've made a personal connection with over an extended period of time though.

One Time

- **Set up your LinkedIn account** and go through all the steps of completing your profile. This is where people find out who you are and what you do. Be specific.

- **Add some connections**. Start with some other writers you actually know. Maybe it's someone from your local writing group, your critique partners, or somebody you chat with all the time on Twitter. LinkedIn will start suggesting other people you may know that are connections of your connections.

- **Join a group**. There are quite a few writers' groups. Search for one that is active and has writers in it that publish or want to publish the same way as you. You may even be able to find a group that also writes the same genre. Or look for groups with members who have common professional interests with you besides writing.

Every Once in a While

- **Add some more connections.** Hopefully you're being social and making real connections with people. Add them. Check the connections of your connections. See if there is anyone in there you might know.

- **Endorse some of your connections'** skills and expertise. Click on any of your connections and scroll down to their skills and expertise. Then click that little plus sign for anything you know they do well. Once you have endorsed a few people, LinkedIn will ask you to endorse other people and their skills. A box will likely pop up when you check your profile to ask you to endorse others. Click away. Endorsements have a reciprocal culture in LinkedIn. The more people you endorse, the more endorsements you'll get.

Social Media Barista

Start your own group on LinkedIn. The best part of this social media platform is finding great content on writing and then connecting to the people who provide that content. If you aren't finding the right group for what you want to talk about related to writing, start your own group. Have some key people in mind to invite to join and spread the word. Then make sure you post interesting and relevant content there.

On your Social Media Coffee Breaks

Remember, LinkedIn is not Facebook.

- **Post new content**, but not what you're having for lunch today or the cute picture/video of your cat playing with your laser pointer. And especially don't start spamming people with links to buy your book or asking people to promo for you.

  This is the place to post articles on writing, marketing, or publishing. This is the place to find speakers for your local writing chapter's conferences. This is the place to learn about your industry and help other authors learn about it too. You can build amazing professional connections and references here. So post appropriately.

- **Post an article** you've found that relates to writing or your genre. Endorse someone's skills, add a new connection. Comment in one of your groups. Start a new thread in one of your groups. One of the greatest ways to get people to respond to your threads in the groups is to ask a question. People love to give advice and you just may learn something new.

Tumblr

Tumblr is a great alternative to Facebook and blogging because it's kind of both combined. It's more than just an FB update, but not quite as formal as a blog. Like many other social media networks, you'll follow people and they'll follow you. I've seen authors who use this as their primary platform, making it look like their website and blog. Most Tumblr blogs are very image heavy (and a favorite of photo bloggers), so if you love to post pictures but want to save your words for your current WIP, this is the place for you.

Pros

- Tumblrs are really great at reblogging content they like, and your posts can very easily go viral.
- Tumblr has some fun features that other blogs don't have, like the reblog button, phone-in audio blogs, and you can make (using something like Photoshop) those fun, animated GIFs from video. I love those things.
- Tumblr blogs are well known for being innovative and interesting. If that's you, this is the place to be.

Cons

- You can get lost for hours checking out other blogs. I laughed for a half an hour checking out dogs (and cats) who've been shamed by their owners while I was in the middle of writing this chapter. Oops.

- It's a little harder to use this as your primary platform since it isn't as formal as a website or regular blog.
- There isn't as much interaction. This is problematic if this is your primary platform as it's harder to make those personal connections.

One Time

Set up your account and choose a theme. I had a hard time doing any sort of uploading of my own theme, although I'm sure it's doable. Choose something that reflects you and your brand.

Every Once in a While

- **Follow other Tumblr blogs**. Find people and content you like and that relates to you and your writing. Check out Tumblr.com/explore. This is a great place to find blogs you might like.

- **Blog**. This is just like any other blogging platform, so you don't have to post every day. You may want to do it more than once a week, though, since Tumblr is somewhere in between a blog and other social media sites, but you don't have to. Once a week is still a great timeframe.

Social Media Barista

- **A webpage from your Tumbls.** If your Tumblr blog has gone viral, think about starting a webpage for the same content. Or vice versa. If you've got great content of the kind that goes viral, think about Tumbling it.

- **Get people to submit content for your blog.** For a great example (and lots of belly laughing), check out one of my fave Tumblr blog, *Dog Shaming*.

On your Social Media Coffee Breaks

- **Check out the other Tumblrs** you follow and reblog them with your own comments.

- **Share Tumblrs** you like on your other social media platforms, like Facebook and Twitter. Share the love.

Foursquare

This social media network is great if you go to a lot of places, like restaurants, and want to share where you're located. I don't recommend this as a primary or even a secondary platform, unless you're a travel writer. This one is best for a tertiary. You can best use this to just add a little spice to your other platforms.

Pros

- It's super easy if you have a smart phone and it only takes seconds to check in (depending on how fast your phone takes to get you on the web).
- It's fun to let your readers know if you're in a location where your books takes place.

Cons

- Unless you're a food critic/travel writer/some job where people care where you are, people may not really care where you are at any moment of the day.
- You could get a stalker. Foursquare friends can see your GPS location and hunt you down.

One Time

Sign up for an account. Fill out your whole profile, including your picture. Get the app for your smartphone and link your account to your other platforms (like Facebook or Twitter). Check to see if any of your social media friends are already on and add them as friends.

Every Once in a While

Share tips at favorite places. Tell your Foursquare friends what your favorite dish or drink is at a hot spot you frequent. Anything that is engaging content. My all-time favorite tip was at a library where I often write (and was the mayor of for a while) that commented on the beautylisciousness of the librarians. Good tip.

Social Media Barista

- **Become the mayor** of a place you frequent. If you go to the same Starbucks, library, or bookstore every day to write, that's something people would like to know about you. Check in there every time and when you've checked in more than anyone else, you become the mayor. Yay! Also, as a personal perk many businesses offer discounts and freebies to mayors and sometimes even for checking in.

- **Develop a top-twelve list**. These are places you frequent or where you love to hang out. You can also check out other people's lists and add the places and suggestions to your to-do list.

- **Have a foursquare scavenger hunt**. Plan a "meet the author" event using Foursquare. You can do this with a top-twelve list or if you're at a reader's conference. Check-in at several locations on the way to the event and have your fans figure out where you are going, and let them come find you!

On your Social Media Coffee Breaks

Check in somewhere your readers or friends will find interesting. You should add a shout-out with the check-in. These should be little comments that your readers and fans will find interesting. Good examples include, "I'm here to finish the book today!" Or, "My character [name] would love this bar!"

GetGlue

Do you (or a character you write) like to watch TV? How about movies? Then GetGlue is the place for you (to add some extra content to your primary platforms). When you're watching a show or a movie, you check in, earn badges, and interact with other people who are also watching the show. The reason I like this one over, say, Miso, is because they got it figured out when it comes to rewards. When you watch shows and check in, you earn stickers. Unlike most other virtual rewards, GetGlue figured out a way to bring the virtual into reality. After you've earned twenty stickers, or once a month, you can get actual stickers sent to you. Cool.

If you use this network, be sure to link it to Facebook or Twitter (or the like) so your fans there can see how you spend your time when you aren't writing.

Pros

Lots of people who read also watch TV. Really. And they often watch in the same genre they read. You might attract some new fans when word gets around that you write stories similar to their favorite TV show.

Cons

This network isn't very big yet, and it's pretty exclusive to TV watchers. Some of those people don't even read books.

One Time

Set up an account, choose some of your favorite shows, set up your TV service provider, and set up the rest of your profile. Use Facebook and Twitter to see if any of your other friends are also on GetGlue.

Every Once in a While

- **Order the stickers** you've earned. If you have some readers or fans that are just as into the shows as you are, give those stickers away!

- **Friend a few people** who watch the same shows you do.

Social Media Barista

Add some clips and pictures from your favorite shows. Got any good gossip about the stars? This is the place to talk about it.

On your Social Media Coffee Breaks

Check in. Whenever you're watching one of your favorite shows, check in. See who else is checking in for this show and comment about what you are (or are not) enjoying about this episode.

MySpace

Oy vey. The death of the original MySpace represented everyone's greatest fears about spending time developing a platform on social media. You work and work and sweat over your computer to give your fans great content and to interact with people and nobody cares.

Well, a few years ago Justin Timberlake (I still imagine him as that hipster in The Social Network — "You know what's cool? A billion dollars.") bought MySpace, or rather, a company he owns a great big chunk of did. They redesigned it and relauched it into its hipster, cool-as-a-billion-dollars forum you can join now. A huge part of the culture on the new MySpace is music. So if you write anything having to do with music, this could be a fun place for you. There are also a lot of youngsters, not little kids, but teens, new adults and twenty-somethings, and wish-I-were-still-a-twenty-something on this network. If you happen to write YA or New Adult literature this is a good place for your readers to see you and how cool you are.

Pros

- With a name like JT behind it, you know they are going to put a lot of time and effort into making this social network stand the test of time.
- There are a lot of really cool and creative people on this network. So, if you're cool and creative too, then you'll find many like-minded people to connect with (and who just might like to read your book.)

Cons

- This is really all about music, not writing. Also, there's a lot of promo of JT's new album. Like, all the time.
- People tend to roll their eyes when you say the words "my" and "space." It's hard to get over the stigma associated with a zombie social media network.

One Time

- **Sign up**, fill out your profile, and upload a good-looking background that speaks to your branding. Find some friends and make some connections. The coolest part of this whole process is choosing a profile song.

- **Choose your top eight**. Once you have a few friends on the new MySpace you can choose your top eight. These are the people who have MySpace lives that you love. Choose wisely.

Every Once in a While

- **Find some new friends**, just like you would on any other social media network.
- **Update** your profile song, and update your top eight.

Social Media Barista

- **Build a playlist for your book**. This is a great way for readers to feel connected to you and your book. I love checking out what other authors listen to when they write and what music they think goes with the book. This is the perrrrrrfect place to share the fun.

- **Make a mix**. This is something that is unique, thus far, to the new MySpace. This is like an interactive collage. Put music, pictures, videos, or anything else you want into the mix. It could be great to use as a pseudo inspiration board. And make it public so your fans can see what is inspiring the next great book you're working on. People love that stuff.

On your Social Media Coffee Breaks

- **Many of the same things you would do on Facebook** work on the new MySpace as well. Check out that chapter for ideas. People still want to see pictures and videos, but mostly ones related to music. Those are your best posts on your SMCBs.

- **Share a song**. The cool thing about the new MySpace is the way they've got the hook-up with record labels. It's really easy to find and share music. It's not as easy to do this on most of the other social networks.

Last FM & Spotify

These two apps are music central. If you're into tunes, if you're a hardcore muso, you'll like this site.

Pros

- Last FM has a ton of widgets that allow you to share your tunage across your other social media platforms, like your website, blog, and Facebook.
- They have free legal downloads of music.
- Everybody likes music.
- Spotify makes it really easy to create and share playlists.

Cons

- It's hard to listen to music and read at the same time. (Really, your brain can only do one or the other.)
- All the cool features that make Last FM and Spotify so appealing to the deeply musical geek can make the site a little intimidating to newbies.
- The no-commercial versions cost money.

One Time

Sign up and fill out your profile. Then peruse the tunes and find something you want to listen to.

Every Once in a While

- **Make a playlist.** You can make one for your current WIP, for your latest release, or if you have a backlist, playlists for those.

- **Check out your neighbors.** These are people who listen to the same kind of music you do.

- **Tag the songs you listen to.** You can use the title of your latest release, great writing tunes, and more. Be creative, but know that Last FM uses these tags for recommendations, so you can also use tags that will be useful for someone looking for good music.

Social Media Barista

Cross promotion. If you happen to be into your local music scene, you might consider doing some cross-promotion in the form of an event with another artist. The events you create will automatically show up on the artist's page and you can both sell some copyrighted materials.

On your Social Media Coffee Breaks

- **Share** your current playlist.

- **Ask others for ideas to develop your playlist** for a book you're writing.

- **Comment** on what you're listening to in one of your groups.

Loops

Loops are kind of like the message boards of days gone by. They are mostly email-based now, although there are still some groups that still use boards. Basically this is like an online community where someone posts a message and other people can respond. Yahoo! Groups is a very popular loop service. Your local writing group and any national writing organizations you belong to likely have and use a loop. There are more loops for writers out there than I can count and they cover all genres and aspects of writing and the writing biz. If you don't have a loop, do a Google search and see if you can find one.

The number one thing to remember about loops (and all the other social media) is to be a real person and interact with the other real people that are there. Go ahead, make some cyberspace friends.

Pros

- Loops are a great way to stay current on what is happening in the writing industry. Members are constantly posting info about what is happening to them or asking questions that are real time-relevant.
- Loops can help you get to know a group of people even when you're spread out over time and space. This one is a great resource if you live internationally or don't have any local writing groups.

- If you use this wisely to make great personal connections with the people in your group, a chunk of them just might buy your book.

Cons

- Loops can be time consuming and clutter up your email. If you're on a Yahoo! Group, you have the option to change how often you get emails, but then you're not reacting to the other members very quickly if you only get the daily digest.
- You and the other members often feel obligated to reply to every single person's posts. Loops quickly get cluttered with emails that are of the "Congratulations!" type.
- Loops are easy to set and forget. Too many people post about their blogs or their releases but never actually interact, which ends up looking spammy. You have to contribute valuable content to be a valuable member. And too many people just don't do that.
- Loops, for the most part, are for writers, not readers. Yes, writers read. If they don't, they probably aren't worth their salt 'n peppa. So you do have the potential to sell some books here, but you should also focus on places for readers, not writers.

I don't recommend this as a primary platform. It's more of a way to make friends and stay sane. Keep the amount of loops you belong to in check. I personally can't handle more than about two, or maybe three, before I can't keep up and don't interact with people. You have to decide your own optimum number of loops.

One Time

Find a loop. Your local or national writing organization may have a loop and ask to join it. If not, search Google for writers loops. Post a "hello" letting everyone know you're new to the loop and give them some info about you. If you're already on a loop but haven't been using it, read the past week or so worth of posts to get a sense of what's going on in your organization.

Every Once in a While

Monitor the loops you're on to make sure they are beneficial to you. If it's full of a bunch of spammy "Check out my latest blog interview!" posts and no discussions, it's not worth your time.

Search for a new loop that has relevant content for what you're doing with your writing now. There are loops for marketing, craft, critique partners, self-publishing, fans/readers of a particular genre, and anything else you can think of.

Social Media Barista

Start your own loop. If you're a new author or pre-published think about creating a loop of other authors on something you are either very good at, or that you need help with. I belong to one loop where each of us posts on a rotating schedule some topic we need help. Then everyone else responds. I get some really great information from this group of writers.

Some very successful authors have loops just for their readers. It's a place where fans can interact and go "squeeeeee!" when your next release is coming out. Before you start your own, check out loops of some authors and join them to see how it's done.

On your Social Media Coffee Breaks

Read and respond to three-ish messages on the loop.

If there isn't any interesting content, start a new topic on something you've been wondering about.

YouTube

You didn't really think of this as a social network, did you? The best way to use YouTube is as a supplement to your other social media platforms. But it can be a very powerful tool. People spend way more time watching videos these days than anything else on the Internet. Did you know that YouTube is the second most popular search engine after Google? (Sorry, Bing.)

Pros

- This one is totally visual (and a little audial), so you're reaching out to people in a very different medium. People love to see the real you. This is your chance to let them.
- There are truckloads of people that watch stuff on YouTube every stinking day. The potential to get noticed is huge. See Justin Beiber (you can still watch his original, aren't-I-so-cute-and-talented-you'll-want-to-throw-up video on YouTube.)

Cons

This is a totally different medium. You want me to be on TV? I just write (here in my little book cave).

One Time

Sign up for an account and set up your own YouTube channel. Your channel doesn't have to have any original content if that scares you. You'll add other videos you watch, like, or think your readers will like here, too.

Every Once in a While

Add videos you or your readers and fans will like to any of your blog posts. Interactive media has a much higher rate of engagement and keeps people on your website or blog a lot longer (giving them time to say, "Hey, there's a new book I'd like to read.").

Social Media Barista

Bring it on. You're photogenic, your screen test was brilliant, and you know how to make love to the camera. It's your turn. Lights, camera, action!

- **Google+.** Remember the section a few pages ago on Google+? This is where you can upload Google Hangouts. Great promotional tool!

- **Vlog**. It's like a blog, but on video. This can be anything from just running journal-style commentary, to funny skits you and your cohorts make, while acting out scenes from your latest release. I've also seen some great writing-how-to or writing tips videos done by authors. If your audience is authors, great idea. If other writers aren't your target reader, try making a how-to video on some topic from your book. You don't have to write nonfiction to do this either.

- **Make a video about whatever you're researching**.

  You're a writer. You probably researched something to write your story. Tell us about what you discovered. Did you write a Regency romance? I'll bet you learned all about old English underpants. Your readers will be fascinated by that. Trust me. Did you write a thriller/horror/suspense with a knife-wielding serial killer? Why don't you do a how-to on surviving knife wounds? This will be infinitely more interesting to your fans and readers than a how-to on eliminating the passive voice from your writing or how to market your book using social media!

- **Upload trailers for your books**. These are like commercials, but movie style. There's tons of software out there to make these trailers yourself, like PowerPoint, iMovie, Windows Movie Maker, and many more. You may already have some movie-making software on your computer now. There are also many companies that will make a trailer for you. Google it. There will be pages and pages.

Before you decide to do a book trailer, pop onto YouTube and search for book trailers. Watch a lot of them and choose a few you like. See what elements of them speak to you and make you want to read and/or buy that book. Emulate those. Choose a few you really don't like and identify what turned you off. There are too many bad book trailers out there and so many are pretty much identical. Be creative. Don't be the same-same-but-different author. Be the cutting-edge-getting-noticed author.

One of the best trailers I have ever seen was simply a well-formatted interview with an author talking about why she was so excited to write this book, which then ended with the information on how and where to get her book. It certainly wasn't in a genre I normally read or am even interested, but darn tootin', I bought it. It was pretty good.

On your Social Media Coffee Breaks

Watch some videos and add them to your channel.

Share the videos you watch on your other social media platforms.

Instagram

If you like to take photos, you might like Instagram. It's all about sharing your life with your friends (or readers and fans) through pictures. It's kind of like Pinterest, but different because you are encouraged to post your own photos. It's also rampant among the younger generation. For teens, this social media network is hotter than a fireman on the fourth of July. So if you write YA, be here.

Instagram was acquired by Facebook a while back, so it's really easy to integrate with FB and will add a little something extra, if FB is one of your primary or secondary platforms. You might also pin your pictures to Pinterest if you're using that too.

Pros

Instagram users are very active. There's a lot of interaction. This network is more social than Pinterest. People do a lot of commenting on pictures and there have even been stories of people finding their happily-ever-afters on Instagram. The official Instagram for Business blog has a story of two photographers who liked the other's pictures and now they like each other. Cute.

Cons

A picture may be worth a thousand words but, um, you're a writer, you use words. It's going to be harder

for you to come up with what to post. Especially if you
don't take pictures or don't have a smartphone.

One Time

- **Sign up for an account** and fill out your profile. You
  may want to try the desktop version of Instagram
  and/or viewers like Extragram. Get the app on your
  smartphone. This makes it easy to take and share
  pictures, which is the point.
- **Get the smartphone app.** Out of all the social media
  networks in the book Instagram is the best one to have
  on your phone. They make it really easy to take pictures
  and upload them right away.

Every Once in a While

**Surf through the pictures and follow some new
people** who have interesting content.

Social Media Barista

- **Have a photo contest.** There are similar ideas in the
  chapter on Pinterest.

- **How it's made.** One of the popular themes for
  businesses (and yes, you are a business) is to tell "how

it's made" stories through pictures. This could be especially fun if you're a self-pubber because you are intimately involved in the how it's made after the manuscript is finished.

On your Social Media Coffee Breaks

- **Post some pictures**. Some ideas for what to post are: Book covers, inspirations for your current WIP, and you (not just writing, but maybe when you're out researching something for your book, traveling, or hanging out with other authors). Remember, you're sharing and telling about your life (or your story) through pictures. Engage with people by asking questions in your caption. Be sure to use #hashtags here just like you would on Twitter. It helps people find your pictures easier.

- **Comment on other people's photos**. This is how you interact with people on this network, so be social.

Vine

Vine is to YouTube what Twitter is to Facebook. That is to say a shorter, funnier version. If you didn't understand any of that SATesque comparison, Vine is the Danny DeVito to YouTube's Arnold Schwarzenegger.

If you're intimidated by a ten-minute video, you might like the mini-format of Vine. All you get is six seconds. It's amazing what fun you can fit into that short amount of time. (My personal favorite is the guy who uses his cat as a machine gun. Cracks me up every time. Also, it doesn't work on my cat).

The teenagers are crazy-mad for this newest social media network. It gives them and anyone else six seconds to just be weird. And they are. So once again, if you write YA or New Adult, this is the place to be.

Pros

- It's fun. And funny. If you write comedy or have a good sense of humor, this is your place to shine.
- Vine is a great place to let your fans put a face to a name. Let them see the slightly strange everyday you. Let your freak flag shine, baby.
- The content of your Vines is as endless as your imagination. You can make videos on everything from strange items on a menu to music videos.
- It requires very little work. About ten seconds' worth. Two to figure out what you want to Vine about, six-ish to record a video, and two to post it.

Cons

- You, uh, have to be in some videos. This might be harder if you're camera-shy, but not impossible. Think stop-motion with inanimate objects.

- Vine is in its just-back-from-the-honeymoon phase and there are lots of spammers trying to find a way to make a buck off the latest and greatest craze. It will take work to ignore and avoid them for a little while. Eventually the spammers will become white noise like on all of our other social networks.

- You have to be funny or interesting (or just plain crazy-weird). No posts about what you had for breakfast (unless you're dining with Prince Harry and eating sparkly unicorn crumpets).

- This app is only available for smartphones and some tablets. As of now there is no desktop application. Gotta have the new-fangled gadgets for this one.

One Time

- **Sign up** for an account and fill out your profile.

- **Get the app** on your smartphone or tablet.

Every Once in a While

Surf through the videos and follow some new people who have interesting content. Check out what fun new hashtags people have come up with and note any that might work for you.

Social Media Barista

- **Have a Vine contest**. There are similar ideas in the chapter on Pinterest, just apply them to videos instead of pictures.

- **Make a Vine book trailer**. You only have six seconds to tell us all about your story. It could be infinitely funny. Don't be boring here. No, "Here's my new book, buy it please"-and-flash-the-cover. I'd recommend some reenactments (but not of your erotica). Try using Barbies and Lego men. Ha, ha, ha. See, I'm laughing already.

On your Social Media Coffee Breaks

- **Revine**. Scroll through the videos and re-Vine and comment on a few of the ones you like. Follow some of the Viners who have content you enjoyed.

- **Search some topics** you're interested in. I bet there are Vines about almost anything you can think of. Fear and hatred of bees, laughing babies, giant dandelions, etc. And if there aren't any videos on a particular topic, well, make one.

- **Check out trending hashtags.** One of my personal faves is #6secondScience. If you can create a hashtag like that for writers, I will be your best friend.

- **Make a video.** About anything. Be funny, be interesting, be bizarre. Just be you. Then post it. Vine is hashtag happy and (unlike Twitter) it's perfectly okay to put a slew of them in your video description.

- **Share on your other networks.** The Vine people make it really easy to share on Facebook and Twitter straight from the app. So if you use one of these platforms, go for it.

CHAPTER 9

Triberr:
The Blogapalooza

Yes, there is another chapter on social media tools, but Triberr is such a revolution, and is used so poorly by most people, that I figured it needed its own diaTribe/explanation. If you blog, and you're on Twitter, this is a great tool for you. This isn't exactly a social network, but a way to help you use your social platforms easily and more effectively.

The basics of this tool is that you join Tribes of people who blog about interests similar to yours. When you post a blog, it will upload to your Tribe's feeds. Your Tribemates then approve your posts to go out on their social media platforms, namely Twitter and Facebook. Anytime your Tribemates blog, their posts are put into your feed for you to approve and get out onto your social media platforms. This is the ultimate way to support other authors on social media.

Once you approve a post, Triberr will tweet and/or post it for you. You don't have to do a thing, just wait for it to pop up in your stream. The default is set to send out one post every twenty minutes until it gets through all of your approvals.

Now, be very careful here. I'm not saying you should approve a bunch of posts and walk away letting Triberr just automate your whole social media day. Only approve posts when you are going to be online anyway. Read more about this in the Social Media Coffee Break section of this chapter. I'll show you exactly what to do to use this effectively and not get spammy. My advice on how to use this tool is not exactly the current MO for Triberr users. So beware. Until you get your Tribemates to see the light of Coffee Break Social Media, you may get kicked out of a few Tribes.

Pros

- You can make amazing connections with your Tribemates. These people are supporting you and your writing and you're supporting theirs. These authors can become your biggest fans.
- If you don't have time to peruse a ton of blogs every day for great articles on writing, book promotion, and new releases of books in your genre, Triberr is your timesaver. You'll have great content readily available, if you choose wisely when joining Tribes or forming your own.

Cons

- It's easy to get lazy and just automate a bunch, of approvals and let it tweet while you're not even paying attention. Bad author. Bad, bad author.

- If your Tribes grow too big or you join too many, you can get overwhelmed with the amount of posts to approve. And then you'll get lazy in your support and your socializing.
- Most of your Tribemates won't be as social-media savvy as you are (after reading this book) and they might not use Triberr well. You don't want your content becoming spam from someone else. You'll have to train these people up.

One Time

- **Sign up for Triberr** and link your blog and social media platforms. (Triberr walks you through how to do this. If you still don't have it figured out afterward, Google it.)

- **Grow your Tribe.** Decide what kind of people you want to attract to your tribe (you automatically are the Chief of one tribe—your own) and write a good blurb about what kind of bloggers you are looking to add to your Tribe. Invite some people to join your Tribe. Be selective. If you can start with some writing friends, that's best. This way you can make sure they know what they are doing, or you can help guide them in the best practices for Triberr.

- **Check the Bonfires** for other Tribemates and to look for Tribes you might want to join. Again, be selective in the Tribes you join. And please, please, don't join more than a couple. With up to sixty Tribemates you could potentially get sixty blogs to tweet or post every day. Ugh. That's not gonna work. Hopefully you have smart Tribemates who don't feel like they have to blog every single day. This way you get some great new content every day and not thousands of the same old, same old.

Every Once in a While

- **Check in with your people by commenting on your Tribe's page.** This is a great place to let them know about your upcoming blog tour. You could even organize one with them. A couple of my Tribemates have side businesses that relate to the writing world and will offer special deals, like book covers or editing, to the people in their tribes first as a perk for supporting them. Do that if you can.

- **Edit your Tribes.** If you have a tribemate that isn't active, hasn't approved anyone's posts for a month or so, and hasn't blogged either, it's a good bet they've dropped this part of their social media plan. Send them a message first to check in, but if you don't get a response in a reasonable amount of time you might need to chop them from your Tribe.

- **Add someone new to your Tribe**. Find someone with great content that you and your readers and followers will find interesting and ask them to join. You may also check with bloggers or friends outside of Triberr and ask if they'd like to join you on this social media tool.

On your Social Media Coffee Breaks

- **Log in**. You should try to log into Triberr at least once a day if you can. If you really can't make it more than once every few days, then make sure to let your Tribemates know that you'll only be approving about once a week.

- **Check out your stream**. I always do a quick scroll through and open up any blogs I actually want to read. Click on the URL below the blog post to open up the actual blog. If you have time, read and post a comment on the blogs you really enjoy. Show some love.

- **Approve posts**. Now head back to Triberr and decide which posts you want to approve. You do not have to approve everything. If a post doesn't appeal to you or your followers, do not approve it. Do not. It's okay, you won't hurt any savvy Tribemate's feelings. I have one Tribemate in a Tribe I joined a while back who just doesn't blog about anything that interests me in the least. I think I've only ever approved one of his blog posts. It's all good. He probably doesn't really read my blog so much either. Delete the posts you aren't interested in.

Now you're left with the blogs that you want to share. Don't hit that approve button yet (or even hover over it). Here's where your social media smarts come into play. You are going to update the title of the post. Remember when I told you your blog titles should be interesting? This is why that's important.

If I tweet something that says "author interview [a link] via @twitteruser," not so many people are going to click on that link or retweet or engage with me. At all. But lots of bloggers call their blog posts something like that. Ugh. YOU need to change this to something interesting and you also need to comment. What you see in that blog title is exactly what will appear in the tweet or Facebook post. Now is the time to engage with your tribemate. Comment and change. Here's a revision of the above:

Congrats on your USA Today interview, [Tweeter]! Woot! RT: I'm a USA Today author! Read the interview here [a link] via @twitteruser

Now, am I actually retweeting this post? No, not technically. But my followers don't need to know that.

And, I've engaged with my friend Tweeter. (She's very active on Twitter — lol.) You can also comment with things like, This is LOL RT:, or Hey thriller fans, read this RT:. Anything you want that helps you interact with your followers and Tribemates.

CHAPTER 10

_____

Social Media Tools: Help Me, Help You

A long with the explosion of social media websites has been the supernova of tools to help you use, analyze, and enhance your platforms. There's everything from programs to make your profiles pretty to websites to monitor whether your efforts are actually doing anything.

Do a search for social media tools and you'll get a bazillion results. The best are the articles where someone explains which tools they use and why. I've found most of the good ones I like by word of mouth and blogs. I'm a big fan of free, so the tools I'm sharing here are all of the no-dinero kind. You don't need to pay for any social media tools, unless you are a highly profitable company. And if you are pulling in the big bacon, let your PR firm pay for those tools and bill you.

Here are the tools I like to use.

For All your Social Media Platforms
A Graphic Designer

I am not a graphic designer, unless you count Facegoo on my iPhone. I tried a free trial of that fancy photo/picture editor once and I think it was more frustrated with me than I was with it. Unless you are picture-editing savvy or have a degree in technology and art, I recommend hiring someone to create your Facebook landing page, Twitter header and background, and website graphics (like your background, header, logo etc.).

I'm a fan of free and the ability to do things for yourself. Sure you can mess around and create something for yourself for free. And you might even think it looks pretty schnazzy. But it is possible everyone else thinks your four-year-old did it. All those super fun fonts with the shadows and shapes that match your brand so perfectly just make your stuff hard to read. I could go on and on about the poorly designed blogs I've seen. So do yourself a favor, skip the high-end coffee for a couple of weeks and hire someone professional to do your graphics for you.

Find these graphics gurus online, in your local writing group, Craigslist, Fiverr, or recommendations from other authors who have sites or profiles you think look groovy. Contact them — it's an actual human interaction to say, "Hey, your website/Facebook page/Twitter profile look great. Who did your graphics?"

For your Website/Blog

SEO

If you're using Wordpress for your website/blog, you neeeeeeeed the plug-in (read: extra special tool) called All-In-One SEO Pack. SEO is Search Engine Optimization. Google and Bing and any other search engine you may use looks at key words and metadata (read: special website/blog stuff) to help its users find what they are looking for. If you Google your name, you sure as heck want your website and other social media platforms to pop up in those results. The way to do that is through SEO. This plug-in helps get the right keywords and metadata (aka stuff on your blog) so the search engines find you, and not Amy Adams wearing some new denim jeans.

If you're still not using Wordpress there may be plug-ins for your platform. Google it. Hopefully the plug-in creators used good SEO.

The Google Analytics plug-in makes analyzing where your website traffic is coming from easier than sliced bread. More on this in Tools to see if your efforts are worth it.

For Facebook and/or Twitter

Tweetdeck/Hootsuite/Janetter

One of my fave tools for FB and Twitter is Tweetdeck. It makes it so much easier to see what is going on if you're using these social media networks. One of the biggest complaints/fears from social media newbies and oldbies alike is the sheer volume of stuff to look at on the Facebook or Twitter homepage. This will help you fix that. Tweetdeck (or its cousin Hootsuite, or the red-headed stepchild-cum-genius protégé Janetter) are programs called user client applications that you will download to your computer.

If you want to be able to see what's most important to you, and not the millions of tweets flying by so fast you can't even read them, use Tweetdeck to create some columns using hashtags.

For example, I'm much more motivated to write when I'm doing it with someone else. But the writer's life is often solitary. So when I'm holed up in my book cave, I can hop on the hashtag #1K1hr and see who else wants to (try to) write one thousand words in an hour. This is a permanent column in my Tweetdeck.

You can also organize by people. You'll need to set up groups first to do this. I have a column for agents and editors I'm following. It helps me keep my pulse on the finger of publishing.

I'll admit this one is more useful for Twitter users, but you can also see your Facebook stream in a column here too.

Here's the controversial part of Tweetdeck: Automation.

You can schedule tweets or FB posts to go out at a pre-determined time. This can be good if you use it well. It can be disastrous if you use it to become a spamming lame-o. Don't be a lame-o.

Use the scheduler for times you are going to be on social media anyway. Maybe you're doing a series of funny quotes as promotion for your upcoming book release. Go ahead and schedule those, but beware if you aren't online and you tweet something at an inappropriate time, say like during a terrorist attack, or you'll be the one to get attacked. Don't believe me? Google the Kardashians and the Boston bombings. Yikes. Essentially they (or their PR firm) tweeted some promotional tweets that were funny and snarky and meant to look like they were personal and actually online. And they were scheduled to tweet out all day long on April 15, 2013. Oops.

The other problem with automation is if someone replies to your tweet and you're not there to reply back. That's just gross of you. So I'm just saying, use it if you want — but be very careful with it.

Buffer

This little app is the best invention for people who look at stuff on the Internet and use social media. Say you're looking at a great article on how to prepare for the zombie apocalypse and you'd love to share it on FB or Twitter. But, what a hassle to have to copy the website link, go over to Facebook, write the post, and then copy the link all the while hoping you don't accidentally close the website or something.

Instead, try Buffer. Go to their website, sign up, and then download a plug-in (special website tool) for your browser. I'm a Chrome fan because plug-ins are so easy to manage with Chrome. The plug-in will put a little button up in your browser bar that looks like three black books stacked on top of each other. Now anytime you're on a cool website, reading an article online, or see a funny pic, you'll click that button and a dialog box will pop up right there on your screen. You decide where you want to post (Twitter or FB or both) and say what you want to say. Then send it out now. No switching websites, no copy and pasting. Just good clean sharing.

There is also the choice to buffer the post, which means schedule it for later. See the section above on scheduling posts and tweets to decide what to do.

TwitterCounter/Qwitter/Manage Flitter

If Twitter is your primary social media crack, uh, platform, you'll find these three tools invaluable. TwitterCounter does exactly what it says: it counts how many everything on Twitter — how many followers and how many tweets you've sent. It has some premium services too, but don't bother with those.

Qwitter helps you see who unfollows you. It will send you a periodic email telling you how many people have unfollowed you recently and who some of them are. If it's just spammers unfollowing you, no worries. But if a slew of other authors and readers have unfollowed you beware. Check what you've been tweeting in the last week and see if you've either been behaving badly (hopefully unwittingly) or have been spammy. Remember that ten-to-one ratio and you should be fine.

Manage Flitter is a great tool for unfollowing people yourself. It can sort by fake followers, people who aren't active, and even people who are spammy. Do unfollow people who aren't useful and interesting, but don't use their handy feature that lets you tweet how many people you've unfollowed. That's just rude.

There is one tool not to use on FB and Twitter. Do. Not. Ever. Pay. For. Followers. Ugh. Even thinking about it gives me the shivers. Don't use the "get followers" services. They do not provide the followers you want, aka real people. I promise.

Across Multiple Platforms

If This Then That

Superfun app. Look up IFTTT to get it. I will here and now admit two things. One, I'm a Star Wars geek. Two, I have one scheduled Facebook post/Tweet set up in IFTTT. Every May 4 "I" post "May the fourth be with you."

But this application is really useful for all kinds of things. Its main purpose is to do stuff automatically for you. For example: See above. But it can also do some timesavers. If you change your Facebook profile picture it will automatically update your Twitter profile picture. If you want a reminder to write texted to your phone every day, IFTTT can do that too.

One of the things I find fascinating about this application is all the new and interesting social media tools and platforms I discover and new ways to use them. Surf through the recipes, pick a few that are useful for you and check out some great new way to use your social media and tools while you're at it.

Gravatar

This is the one social media tool I wish someone had told me about years ago. Hopefully you've been convinced to get a professional headshot and use the heck out of it. An avatar is that little picture of you we see online everywhere.

A great way to use that pretty mug for author branding is when you comment on blogs. If you use or comment on a Wordpress blog/website (or any other site using Gravatar), your picture will appear next to the comment instead of the weird snowflake or cartoon character. All you have to do is sign up for the service and upload a pic. They'll do the rest.

Pic Monkey

You remember that photos up the coolness factor of your content, right? Good. Personalizing your photos with text and fun stuff makes your cool go through the roof. There are lots of sites out there to edit photos. Pic Monkey is just one that is free, easy to use, and there is no registration required. They also have a share button so you can go straight from their website to your platforms or you can save your pics to your computer too.

Choose a picture you want to use on your social media, blog, Facebook, etc., and upload it to the PicMonkey page. I don't always have a picture I want/need to use and I don't want to get sued for using some copyrighted material. What's a writer to do? Well, you can buy some stock photography (there are a few places that have free stock photos too – just Google it) or you can try Flickr. This is a photography social media site where people upload pictures they have taken to share with the world. You can search for images to use that have Creative Commons licenses. Be sure to check what kind of rights there are on a picture before you download it. Sometimes you just need to attribute the photographer. Which is easy to use if you slap some text on your picture that says something like: Photo Credit: Their Name.

Newsletters

First, a word about newsletters. You probably want to have one. There are lots and lots of opinions on how to do them and the power of using them effectively to sell more books. I recommend having one and making sure there is a sign up on your website for it. The people who sign up for your newsletter (unless you've coerced them into it with a poorly designed contest) are actually interested in you and your writing. Plus, the bonus kicker, they are actually asking you to make sure they know about when you do something noteworthy. Think about sending it out only to announce really big stuff, like say, book releases. Think about signing up for the newsletter of some authors you love and see what they do. I don't recommend sending one out weekly, monthly, or quarterly just because you want to keep up with your fans. That's what the rest of your social media is for.

Mail Chimp

There are a few newsletter services out there for you to choose from. I like Mail Chimp because it's free for up to a couple thousand subscribers, it's easy to use, and they have free templates and some great analytics. They even provide templates where you can upload pictures, insert pretty-colored headlines, and links to your books.

Tools To See If Your Efforts are Doing You Any Good

Even using the Coffee Break mentality, you'll still put some of your valuable time and effort into building your platform with social media. So how do you know what's working and what's a waste of time? Analytics.

It's not scary, I promise. Numbers savants and Excel gurus could spend all their time examining and mining the info for data. For the rest of us, it gives a clue on if we're doing it right.

Klout

This straightforward website takes a look at your online presence via the social media sites you use and tells you simply and clearly how cool you are. They give you a score out of 100. People like Justin Beiber are (unbelievably) at the top of the chart and your grandma is somewhere around zero.

Sign up for a Klout account now and see how your score grows over time. Authors who have spent a little time working on their social media platform are usually in the forties. Those who really rock it are in the sixties.

One of the best features is the Your Moments page. I'm surprised most every time I check out my Moments to see what's been uber-popular. Wine usually gets a win.

Link Shorteners

If you include a link to anything of yours — website, blog post, your book page on Amazon — you can use a link shortener to shorten the length of the link and track how many clicks you get on it. You can even use these in the back of your self-published book to see if readers click after they finish your story. Bit.ly is my personal fave because it connects with Tweetdeck. It's easy to use and the results are very clear.

If you want to get really fancy you can use a different link that you create through Bit.ly to track how many hits you get for the same thing but that you share on different platforms. Then you'll know which one is the most effective.

You definitely want to do this when it comes to marketing your book. But that's a whole book in and of itself.

Google Analytics

Wanna know how people are getting to your website? (Because you have a website now, right? RIGHT?!) Google Analytics will tell you way more than you ever needed to know.

This is the motherload of analytics for your website. It's also pretty intimidating. You need to understand how to access the code on your website so you can insert a tracking device. It's all very cloak-and-dagger.

But guess what? Wordpress has a plug-in that does it for you. Bwa, ha, ha, ha, ha. Otherwise, I hope you have a webmaster or mistress to help you with this.

Amazon affiliate account

We all know that a kazillion books are bought through the thing that is Amazon. So why don't you get a little piece of the action? Sign up for an Amazon affiliate account. (Not available in some states, but there's ways around that. Shhhh. You didn't hear that from me.) What is this manna from the heavens? You put a link to a book (or product) on your website and if someone clicks on that link and then buys that item, you get a portion of the sale.

Now, I'm not saying you should monetize your author website. In fact, don't. Ads are bad on an author website. But do sell your own books via Amazon and other e-tailers on your website. Also, if you happen to blog about a certain book you liked and use your Amazon Affiliate account for the link to buy, well, then, yay for you and that other author.

Definitely use a link-shortener (like Bit.ly) that can track the clicks from your website (or links in your ebook) to Amazon. You'll be able to see how much traffic you drive from your promotion efforts to sales.

CHAPTER 11

What Works Well Together

You may have read only a few selected chapters of this book. Good for you if you did. Reading the whole thing just might overwhelm and scare you away from social media. But by reading only select parts you might have missed some awesomeness. There are certain platforms that work really well when used together. Check for your platform and then think about adding some of the networks that work well as your secondary or tertiary platforms.

What Works Well with your Website/Blog

It's pretty darn easy to put your blog posts up on Facebook, Google+, and LinkedIn. Hopefully that will direct traffic back to your home base.

YouTube is awesome. And not just for watching funny videos of cats. Try putting a YouTube video into your blog. Or go crazy and do a vlog (video blog).

Goodreads has all kinds of stuff you can put on your website. Like say, the five-star reviews of your books. It can also automatically upload to your blog any reviews you do.

Amazon. You really, really, really want to have links of where to buy your book on your website. If you're a smarty-smart pants your links will go through your Amazon affiliate account.

What Works Well with Facebook

Instagram is your go-to for taking, editing, and posting cool pictures to Facebook.

YouTube videos are great content on a Facebook page. Even better if you happen to be in that video.

Pic Monkey is another photo editor that works well for customizing photos you put in your posts.

Goodreads can post your reviews and your past, current, and future reading lists directly to your FB page for you.

Foursquare is great if you want all your FB friends to know where you are and be jealous of you.

Get Glue will post automatically to FB for you and tell the whole world (well, seven million people) what you're watching on TV.

Vine will automatically upload your videos to your Facebook page so that you can share that six-second wonder with all your friends.

What Works Well with Twitter

Instagram and Pic Monkey are great for creating personalized pictures for tweeting.

YouTube makes it really easy to share videos on Twitter. Just look for the button on the site.

Triberr, if used correctly, can increase your Twitter presence by a lot-fold.

Pinterest makes it super easy to share your pins on Twitter. Just check that little button at the bottom of the pin.

Foursquare can post automatically to Twitter, making your friends jealous of your whereabouts.

Get Glue will post automatically to Twitter so you and all your tweeps can talk Downton Abbey, The Walking Dead, or other not-as-cool shows you may be watching.

What Works Well with Pinterest

Twitter has a cool relationship with Pinterest so all you have to do is click the little button to tweet your pins. They aren't so kissy face with Facebook.

Use Pic Monkey to make your pictures personalized and kick-ass before you pin them.

What Works Well with Goodreads

Facebook can upload your reading lists and reviews to your homepage automatically. Everyone can know what you're reading today. Fans love that. It can also post your reviews.

Twitter will post a link to any of your reviews if you click the little button.

Amazon bought Goodreads in a super-secret sneaky spy deal sometime in 2013. Who knows what the future of the two together will mean for authors. Keep your eye on it.

CHAPTER 12

See, You Can Do This

The Power is in You

You have the tools and the knowledge now. Go forth and build a prosperous platform. Be sure to wave hello to me. I promise to wave back.

If you read the entire book cover to cover, you're overwhelmed. I hope you didn't do that, but if you did, go back to the chapter on whichever social media network you want to use as your primary platform and read that chapter again. Start there. Don't feel like you need to do anything else until you're ready.

If you're not feeling overwhelmed and you've chosen the social media platforms you want to work with, you may want to put together a social media plan. (You plotters will love this, you pantsers should probably use it to keep yourself organized.)

A Coffee Break Social Media plan will have your primary, secondary, and tertiary platforms listed, what you need to do one time, every once in a while, and on your SMCBs. It also lists the social media tools you'll use. You may also want to keep your passwords, where the platforms are linked to, and a place for notes. If you want a printable version, click on this link to get directed to my website where you can download the forms.

www.coffeebreaksocialmedia.com/books/resources

Example Coffee Break Social Media Plan

Here is an example plan for an author I consulted for.. She chose the platforms she liked and was comfortable with and we put together ideas of what she could do with each of them. Don't copy this plan exactly, but use it as a guideline for your own plan.

Primary Platform — Facebook

One Time

- Look at [NYT Bestselling Author]'s pages (she's a very successful author with several fan pages) to see how she links her different fan pages to her primary profile. Use her as a model.
- Set up your new fan page (linked to your primary profile) and brand them to yourself and your website.
- Hook your pages to your Twitter and LinkedIn accounts, so anytime you post on your page it shows up in those platforms too.

Every Once in a While

- Once a week in the beginning, once a month after that
- Look for and join groups that do the same thing you do (coaching, entrepreneurs, business, women in business, women entrepreneurs, etc.).
- Friend or fan five people, businesses, and groups in your industry/genre.

On your Social Media Coffee Breaks (SMCBs)

Facebook is your primary platform, so it should be your first Social Media Coffee Break, and if you only take one SMCB a day, this should be your platform to do it on.

- Post an update. Something people on FB can interact with or a link to something your followers will find interesting.

- Check out what is going on in one of the groups you've joined and make a comment.
- Like and comment on a couple of people's updates.

Secondary Platform — Twitter

One Time

Update your profile to reflect your brand and platform.

Every Once in a While

When you're comfortable with using and maintaining your Facebook account, start building your Twitter followers. Find an author you like and check out who they follow and who follows them. Choose ten of each and follow them.

On Your Social Media Coffee Breaks

- Check (either on Twitter or Hootsuite) to see if anyone has tweeted you and reply to those people. DON'T just say thanks. DO comment on what they said.
- If you only have a few mentions or none, retweet a few tweets you like and that your followers would like. If you can, comment on those retweets. Example:

  So useful for women entrepreneurs! --> (original tweet)

  Loved this! --> (original tweet)

  This is sooooo me! --> (original tweet) etc.

- Interact with someone. Anyone! Reply to anyone in the stream to get a short conversation going. You may have to try a few people to find someone else who is actually online.

Secondary Platform — Blogging

One Time

- Make a list of 100 things you like. That's what you'll blog about this year (and maybe the next!). Add to this list anytime you like.
- Find out when your industry is on social media and plan to post your blogs just prior to those days. Google "Twitter by industry" and read a few articles to get a good idea for publishing and entrepreneurs. Remember, most people are on SM on the weekends, regardless of industry, and in the morning (when they get to work) during the week. So think about posting your blog on Friday nights, so it will be available all weekend, but still be fresh for those Monday morning entrepreneurs!

Every Once in a While

Only once a week!
- Blog.
- Your blog title should be as interesting as a tweet, short and sweet, but informative. NO more than 100 characters (so people can comment on twitter about it).
  - Tip: You can use hashtags (#) in your blog post title.

On Your Social Media Coffee Breaks

Read and comment on someone else's blog.

Tertiary Platform — LinkedIn

One Time

- Update your profile to reflect yourself and your brand.
- Complete your entire profile and add your picture.

Every Once in a While

- Add anyone you've met at a networking event or conference.
- Endorse 2–5 people.
- Join a group that interests you.

On your Social Media Coffee Breaks

Read the latest posts in one of your groups and comment on one. If there isn't anything of real interest to you, or that you don't feel qualified to talk about, start a new thread of your own. Remember to ask a question to elicit responses and start a conversation.

Social Media Tool — Triberr

One Time

- Sign up for Triberr and link your blog to the account.
- Name your own Tribe and give it a description that signals what your industry is and what you will be blogging about.

- Join a Tribe that has at least five people in it and who blog about things your followers will be interested in. (Don't join more than three tribes. Start with one and ease into it!)

Every Once in a While

- Evaluate whether or not your Tribes are effective. If not, drop them. Then look for a new Tribe to join.
- Invite someone you've met through social media to your tribe.

On Your Social Media Coffee Breaks

- Go through your tribal stream and approve posts that are interesting to you and your followers. Delete posts you don't want to tweet.
- Visit one person's blog that you are interested in and comment on their post.
- Edit 3–5 posts in the stream by commenting on the post and interacting with those people. Examples:

    Congratulations! -->(Tribemates name) RT: (original post)

    Loved this! -->(Tribemates name) RT: (original post)

    Entrepreneurs, read this! -->(Tribemates name) RT: (original post)

- Tip: Feel free to delete promotional posts unless you think your followers would be really interested in them. Don't feel obligated to tweet any particular post, but do try to tweet at least one from each of your Tribemates every week if you can.

Social Media Tool — Buffer

One Time

- Install the Buffer app to your web browser tool bar.
- Link to your Facebook page and Twitter accounts .
- Check out when Buffer thinks is the best time to be on social media and if that works with your schedule. Let it post at those times.
- If not: Set your Buffer schedule (make sure it's when you'll be around to respond!) Better yet. Don't schedule posts, send them now.

Every Once in a While

- When you are online and see something you think your followers or friends would like, hit the buffer tool and send or schedule that link to go out.
  - Tip: Comment on these posts just like you would a Facebook post or tweet you write yourself. Make people interested in clicking on that link!
  - Tip: Buffer will allow you five posts a day for up to three days. If you find more things you want to Buffer than that, save them in a folder in your favorites and visit them at a later date when your Buffer is empty.

Social Media Tool — Klout

One Time

- Join Klout at Klout.com.
- Connect your Facebook, Twitter, LinkedIn, and blog accounts.
- Check your score and make a note of it.

Every Once in a While (about once a month)

- Check your Klout score and make a note if you have increased.
- Surf around the site and look at the info on your interactions and such to get a good idea of what kinds of posts and tweets your network liked and do those kinds again!

Now that you've seen an example it's time to make your own plan.

If you would like a document file (Word or PDF) of this plan template you can visit the Coffee Break Social Media website to download it. www.coffeebreaksocialmedia.com/books/resources

---

Glossary of Social Media Terms

Amazon - noun, 1. An online retailer of goods, including books. 2. The number one seller of books anywhere in the world.

Amazon affiliate – noun, a person who earns money from referring customers to Amazon when they purchase items from Amazon.

Blog (also see **Vlog**) – noun, an online diary. An online place where you let your fans know what's going on in your world.

Coffee Break Mentality – noun, the idea that you don't have to be on social media for long periods of time but can still be engaging, present, and successful at building your online presence while still having time to write.

Co-op money – money paid by a publisher to retailers for prime positioning within the bookstore/book kiosk (like at airports). This is especially for end cap placement, featured books, special displays, and front-facing books.

Download – verb, to take a picture or video from the Internet and put it on your computer.

Email – noun, a form of communication that uses writing and transmitting via the Internet. Verb — emailing

Facebook – noun, a very popular social networking website where you post updates, pictures, videos, and information about you and your books. Verb, to contact someone via the Facebook website or to spend time perusing and posting to the Facebook website.

Flickr – noun, a website and social network based on sharing pictures and images.

Foursquare – noun, a social network based in checking in at places you visit.

GetGlue – noun, a social network based on watching and talking about TV shows and movies.

Goodreads – noun, a social network for people who love books and reading.

Google – noun, 1. An online search engine. 2. A large company that controls a lot of the Internet business in the world. Verb, to Google, to search for information online.

Google+ - noun, a social network owned and operated by Google where users post updates, pictures, videos, links, and more.

Hashtag – noun, the # symbol. Used on social media networks for denoting keywords, to note that your post relates to a specific conversation, or to note that something is significant or funny, or to express a thought. Words following a hashtag are run together and have no punctuation.

Host – noun, a company that uses its computers and servers to make your website available on the Internet. Verb, to have a company use its computers and servers to make your website available on the internet.

Instagram – noun, a website and social network based on sharing photos.

Last FM – noun, a website and social network based on listening and enjoying music.

Link – a URL/ web address for a website. Usually starts with www. Verb, to make social media networks work together so a post on one also shows up on the others.

LinkedIn – noun, a professional social network.

Loops – noun, an online or email forum where users share information with a specific group.

Mail Chimp – noun, a website that helps you create and send newsletters.

MySpace – noun, a social network that died in the 2000s but was then revived and re-invented by Justin Timberlake as a social network for music.

Network – noun, a place on the Internet where you make connections with other people.

Verb – to make connections with people.

Newsletter – noun, a short publication used to send information to and update subscribers on an author's new releases and appearances.

Pin – verb, to share a picture or video on Pinterest.

Noun, the actual picture or video shared on Pinterest.

Pinterest – noun, a website and social media network based on sharing pictures and videos.

Platform – noun, 1. A social media website you socialize on, brand yourself, and let people know about you and your writing. Examples: website, blog, Facebook, Twitter. 2. The information you put out about you and your writing that brands you. Example: A Facebook post with a hot-looking cowboy, a tweet about macaroni and cheese, a blog post about one's favorite iPhone apps.

Plug-in – noun, a tool used on websites like Wordpress to add content or make the site easier to use.

Post – verb, to put content like pictures, videos, writing, etc. on your blog, website, or social network.

Noun, the actual content you have put on your blog, website, or social media network.

Profile – noun, information about you. This usually includes a picture and a short bio.

Retweet – verb, to send a tweet from another user to all of your followers on Twitter. Related: ReVine and RePin.

SEO – noun, an acronym standing for Search Engine Optimization. The concept of using keywords to make your website or content easier to find by search engines such as Google and Bing.

Social media – noun, Internet-based communities where people can interact, post information, pictures, and more. Aka: Your friend. Examples: Facebook, Twitter.

Social Media Barista – noun, a person who is the master of a particular social media network and is ready to do advanced techniques.

Social Media Coffee Breaks (SMCBs) - noun, short five- to fifteen-minute breaks in your writing that you use to be present and engaging on social media.

Social Media Tool – noun, a website or application that helps you be more effective on social media.

Spotify - noun, a website and social network based on listening and enjoying music.

Tribe – noun, a group of users that have joined together for the purpose of sharing each other's blog posts using Triberr.

Triberr – noun, a website for bloggers where they can share content with other members and have their content shared by other members.

Tumblr – noun, a website that is a cross between a blogging site and a social network.

Tweet – verb, to post a message, picture, video, or link on Twitter.

Twitter – noun, an online social network where people communicate using 140 characters or less. Verb, to tweet

Upload – verb, posting things like pictures or videos to a website. Usually requires an extra step and a tool on the website to do it.

Vine – noun, an application that hosts short six-second videos that users produce and upload.

Vlog – noun, a video blog.

Website – noun, 1. That place on the Internet that you call home. 2. The home base to where all of your social media is linked. 3. The place where your fans find all the latest and greatest information about you.

Widget - noun, a tool used on websites like Wordpress to add content, sometimes directly from another website.

Wordpress.com– noun, a website that allows its users to create their own websites and blogs.

Wordpress.org – noun, a website that allows its users to create their own websites and blog using their own URL.

Yahoo! – noun, an Internet company that provides services like email and loops.

YouTube – noun, a website and search engine that hosts videos mostly created by the users.

Your People – noun, the people on social networks that are like-minded to you. They may be fans, writers, friends, family, or other supporters of you and your work.

Resources

If you missed any of the links for resources while reading the book, or are just looking for a quick look at them all, you can find the downloadable files on our website
www.coffeebreaksocialmedia.com/books/resources

Excerpt from

The Coffee Break Guide to Business Plans for Writers

Foreword

When I first started searching for information about writing a business plan all I found was either very formal plans designed for start-up businesses that offered services or products for sale, like you know, sandwiches or cars. A long and tedious report didn't appeal to me, but I wanted something more than just goals. So I took the formal titles and statements, converted them to the kind of work I planned as a writer and created the plot for my work life. That's what you'll find in this book with step-by-step instructions to create your own author business plan.

I'll ask you to consider your goals, think about the way you plan to publish, and where you are at in the publishing journey. In each step I provide ideas and questions you might want to consider for those varying goals. I decided to include them all together so that authors at all phases of publishing might benefit from other perspectives. You might just update and add to your goals by checking out ideas for traditional, self-published, or hybrid authors. Newbie authors can look at multi-published author ideas to help plan their futures and authors who've been publishing for years might get a new perspective on how to get the woo-hoo back in their business.

Additionally, you can write a plan for each book, if you really want to go crazy. I've provided considerations and a generic template to do just that.

Once you've got a good idea of what to include in your goals you might also benefit from running the numbers. Writing is a hard business to figure out how much money you'll actually make, so doing a budget and some projections can help give you a realistic idea.

Throughout the book we've provided links to downloadable documents. If you're reading the e-book you can click on the links. If you're reading the print version all of the links are on the book's page of our website CoffeeBreakSocialMedia.com.

Remember that a business plan is just that, a plan. It should be a living document that you can change as needed, but that should also help hold you accountable to yourself and your business. It's also your life and your work. Not mine, not your father's, yours. You have to decide how much time, effort and thought you are willing to put into it. You also get to choose what you want or need to include. This will vary drastically from person to person, author to author.

Finally, if done all this work to put a plan together, you might want to measure how well you're achieving your goals. The final chapters have ideas on how to do that and (for all you English majors out there) information on budgets, with a downloadable Excel spreadsheet template. It's not that scary, I promise.

So go to it. Make your business plan. Right now. Go.

CHAPTER 1

You Are a Business

Yes, you are a business

Writers write. But in the new age of publishing (that's now) writers have to do a whole lot more than write. They have to establish a platform, market, engage on social media, attend conferences and readers' events, and more. If a writer decides they want to self-publish they also have to create or contract cover art, resource and work with an independent editor, research the market, and stay on top of technological updates. Being a writer is no easy business.

The business of being a writer

That's right. It's a business. The second you decided to get your work published, be it by a traditional publisher or on your own, you became a business. Most of us don't think of our writing efforts in that way. We just write. Right?

I am not an accountant (or a lawyer.) I am a writer. One who has spent years studying the business of writing. Yes we all take classes on craft, do research for our books and have maybe even thought about a marketing plan. We put a whole lot of effort into our books, so why not but that same effort into yourself. You are after all your business's greatest asset. Without you, there is no business.

Unless this is a hobby and the only people who are ever going to read your work are your family and pets then you absolutely are a business. And if you're going to be a business then you're going to want a business plan.

A lot of writers are very right-brained creative people to whom spreadsheets and rows of numbers are like a bad itching powder in your pants. (There are plenty of exceptions to that generalization. Accountants who write romance for example.) And this book has information that you just might want to have a spreadsheet for, but there is also plenty of creative thinking and fluffy rainbows to designing your work life. We are, after all, creating your dream here.

If you are a plotter you're going to love creating a business plan. It will be just like plotting your action/ adventure/ thriller/ romance/ fantasy novel, but better because it's your real life you'll be planning. If you're a pantser we've got plenty for you to do too. Yes, we are going to make you think about your happily ever after and the steps to getting there, but don't worry, you can change it anytime you like.

Why do I need a business plan?

"Writing isn't a business that requires investors or small business loans. What good does a business plan do me?"

You're correct. Writing is not your typical small start-up that requires you to write a proposal with tables and charts to present to your bank or capital venturists so you can get money for your project. (Although some authors do raise funds to support their writing efforts.) The best way a plan can help you is by organizing your goals for your writing career, understand the industry you'll be working in and managing your writing efforts toward success.

"I'm not making any money being a writer, why do I need a business plan?"

Well, I'm glad you asked. First I hope you plan to make some money for all your hard work. You deserve to. Don't get me wrong, you're likely never going to make a katrillion dollars (some people do though) but there are plenty of people out there making a decent living writing. So think positive and plan for it.

"But it takes years to get published. Why do I need a business plan now, why not wait until I sell a book?"

Really? Do you think successful businesses built their plans after they sold their first product? No way. They planned and worked and toiled to make sure that product was the best they could make it and then sent it out into the world hoping someone would produce it, or decided to produce it themselves and then marketed the heck out of their product making all their friends and family members buy it. Sound familiar. It should. That's exactly what writers do. And those businesses had a good solid plan to make that happen.

The Coffee Break Business Plan

Goals are an important part of a business plan

Whatever kind of writing you do and no matter where you are in your path(s) to publishing you have chosen, the best and easiest place to start your plan is with some basic goals. Taking the time to think about what you truly want to do and accomplish with your writing will not only help you put together your strategy, but it will help you focus on actually getting your writing done.

Writers tend to be creative type people by nature, and often we get ideas for our writing from millions of places: dreams, TV shows, newspaper articles, books, real life, everywhere. And when we get these ideas we are excited about them. We want to write these stories down while they are fresh and new in our heads. So many authors get caught in a trap doing just that. They have half a dozen manuscripts started and not a single one finished. You can't sell a book that isn't finished. Sure you might get an advance on a proposal, but if you don't finish writing it, guess what? You have to give all that pretty money back.

By getting yourself straight on what your goals are you can see where you need to concentrate your work. If you don't go all ADHD - look, a squirrel! - in your writing you can get so much accomplished.

If all you ever do on your business plan is set some goals, well, then you're far ahead of most other authors. If you don't finish reading the rest of this book and only write down some of your goals, I'll be a happy camper. But goals are only the beginning, so do keep reading.

A Mini Business Plan

We'll start with a mini version of a business plan and work our way into the big leagues.

Okay, put your thinking cap/top hat/beanie with the helicopter rotor on top/tiara on. It's time to think about what you really want. The answers to these questions will become the basis of your entire plan. These questions are to get you started thinking about your goals, but don't go crazy here and spend hours making lists and/or daydreaming about your success as a writer.

I call this the Coffee Break business plan because you should be able to answer these questions in a coffee break or two.

If this is all you ever do you'll be years ahead of most authors. But since you have this whole book you might keep going and nail down the rest of your plan too. Chapter 5 is all about detailed goals, so spend only a few minutes thinking about each of these questions. Write a couple of sentences to answer them or make yourself a nice bullet-pointed list. If you'd like a template to print out and do this exercise on you can download one at:

www.coffeebreaksocialmedia.com/books/resources

The Coffee Break Business Plan

Get out a pad of paper or start up a new Word document and answer these question for yourself and your writing career.

- How many books do you plan to write and in what genre? What's your projected word count? When will you finish each project? Or how much time will you need to complete each project? (Don't forget about critiques, beta readers, editing and all those other activities besides actually writing the book.)
- How will you publish these books? Traditionally, self-published, a hybrid approach?
- Who is your competition? Who else writes books like yours?
- How will you sell and market your books?
- How much money will it cost you to publish and market? What services might you pay for to help do that?
- How much money do you plan to make and when will you see that revenue?

There you go. You just created a business plan. For real. Laminate that sucker and put it up big and pretty in front of your computer. Every time you sit down to write take a look and focus on writing to achieve those goals. If the IRS comes knocking wave it in their faces.

If you enjoyed this excerpt and would like more help taking control of your writing career by writing a business plan go to www.coffeebreaksocialmedia.com/books to get more information now.

A Thank You From the Author

Dear Reader (who is probably also a writer),

Before you are off to read your next book I wanted to take a quick moment to say thank you for reading this one.

When you go shopping for books to help improve your writing life they are often on the craft of writing, but you chose another direction and took a chance on learning about social media with me. I appreciate that you downloaded and read this book all the way to the end (where you are now).

Remember there are a lot of great free downloadable resources just for readers of this book. If you missed clicking on the links in any chapter, the templates can all be accessed at www.coffeebreaksocialmedia.com/books/resources.

We all know reviews are the king of word-of-mouth marketing. I would be eternally grateful if you would spread the word about The Coffee Break Guide to Social Media for Writers. It will help me understand what you liked, what was useful, and to write more business books for authors like you.

Would you take a minute to leave a review for this book on Amazon?

When you review on Amazon, they will give you the chance to rate the book and share it on Facebook and Twitter. If your writer friends out there in the social-media-o-sphere might like (or need) this book to help them focus their writing life like you have, please let them know about it. Or if you want to get me directly on social media you can find me at:

@AmyDenim on Twitter

Or

www.facebook.com/AuthorAmyDenim

If you liked the content and found the information here useful please let me know. If you have corrections or suggestions for the next version, get those to me too. I love to hear from readers and writers.

Best wishes,

~Amy

ABOUT THE AUTHOR

Amy Denim writes business books for authors and contemporary romance. She loves hot heroes (like chefs and cowboys) and curvy intelligent heroines (like chefs and cowgirls.)

She's been a franchise sales coordinator, a lifeguard, a personal shopper, and a teacher of English as a Foreign Language. But now she spends her days reading and writing at her local library or in her book cave.

XXX

Amy started out her writer's life scared out of her wits because she hadn't yet created an online platform, wasn't on twitter, didn't have a Facebook fanpage and had never even heard of Goodreads. She just wrote books. So she spent a year becoming a social media fiend and now does consulting for creatives on how to use social media effectively. She started Coffee Break Social Media to help writers and artists learn to use SM platforms effectively (without the scare tactics) but still have time to create. She believes social media can be every writer's friend, sometimes they just need an introduction.

Find Amy on most any social media network including:

Facebook: Author Amy Denim

Twitter: @AmyDenim

Pinterest: Amy Denim

Goodreads: Amy Denim

On her website: www.AmyDenim.com

Or at www.CoffeeBreakSocialMedia.com

9006

Made in the USA
Lexington, KY
03 January 2014